Theories of Attachment

An Introduction to Bowlby, Ainsworth, Gerber, Brazelton, Kennell, and Klaus

Carol Garhart Mooney

Redleaf Press®
www.redleafpress.org
800-423-8309

Published by Redleaf Press
10 Yorkton Court
St. Paul, MN 55117
www.redleafpress.org

Photo credits: Photo of Mary Ainsworth courtesy of the Ferdinand Hamburg Archives of The Johns Hopkins University. Photo of John Bowlby courtesy of Sir Richard Bowlby. Photo of T. Berry Brazelton courtesy of the Brazelton Touchpoints Center. Photo of Magda Gerber courtesy of Linda Hinrichs. Photo of John Kennell and Marshall Klaus courtesy of Case Western Reserve University School of Medicine. All photos used with permission.

First edition 2010
Cover design by Mayfly Design
Interior illustration by Erin E. Mooney
Printed in the United States of America
18 17 16 15 14 13 12 11   3 4 5 6 7 8 9 10

Library of Congress Cataloging-in-Publication Data
Mooney, Carol Garhart.
   Theories of attachment : an introduction to Bowlby, Ainsworth, Gerber,
Brazelton, Kennell, and Klaus / Carol Garhart Mooney.
      p. cm.
   Includes bibliographical references and index.
   ISBN 978-1-933653-38-9 (alk. paper)
   1. Infant psychology. 2. Attachment behavior in infants.   I. Title.
BF720.P73M67 2009
155.4'18—dc22   2008043879

Theories of Attachment

Also by Carol Garhart Mooney

Reflections on Parenting (New England AEYC)
Theories of Childhood
Use Your Words

Dedicated with love to my four children,
Sean, Brian, Tom, and Erin

Contents

Acknowledgments

There are always so many people to thank when a book moves from an idea to a reality. The first person I think of in helping me successfully make this transition is my editor, Beth Wallace. Her skill, good humor, professionalism, and patience get me through every time. I thank David Heath and Linda Hein at Redleaf Press for ensuring that editorial relationship, which works so well.

Next I thank my son, Brian Mooney, MHA—"would-be agent" and arranger of international phone calls, hospital tours, and all issues his mom usually struggles with. His knowledge of hospital practice, past and present, has been invaluable to the completion of this text. I also thank his colleagues at Exeter Hospital for showing me how far we have come since I gave birth there decades ago.

I thank my friends Patrice, Joanne, Ann, and Pat for their continual support of my work and their responses to urgent calls whenever I'm not sure what to do next. Their calls, e-mails, flowers, and encouragement keep me going. Their friendships sustain all that I do.

Special thanks are due to Johann Mooney, Lea Janelle Walsh, Stacey Jordan, and Katie Brissette for their honesty and reflection on the role of motherhood in the modern world.

I thank Stacey Jordan, Joanne Parise, Meghan Adams, and LeeAnn McIntyre for modeling expert relations with parents—before becoming parents themselves.

I thank my workplace, The Sisters of Holy Cross, specifically Carol Descoteaux, CSC, General Animator, USA, for valuing the contribution of practical texts to the field of early childhood education and for encouraging my continued attempts to contribute to the field.

The completion of this text has depended on the support of friendships in the early childhood and broader communities of New Hampshire, which have sustained my effort for nearly forty years. The names are too many to list and my fear is I would forget someone, so I'll state only that you know who you are. The New Hampshire tornado of 2008 stole time, records, and energy from this effort that were restored, however, through the tireless efforts and support of my longtime friends Susan Rowe Morison and MaryLou Beaver. Your organization of Early Learning New Hampshire "disaster relief" efforts was extraordinary. For the same reason, I also thank Governor John Lynch for his longtime support of early childhood programs and his specific support of my situation after the storm. My longtime friend Chickie Shanelaris is responsible, once again, for getting my book out. Her efforts have supported every text I've put in print. Each cover bears my name, but it would not have seen print without her!

The final work on this manuscript could not have been completed without the support, skill, and sensible suggestions of Kyra Ostendorf at Redleaf Press. I am truly grateful.

I thank my friend, colleague, and moral compass, Yvette Robert, CSC, for her stories, prayers, jokes, and guidance, without which this work would not have been accomplished.

Finally, I thank my family, who always lead the line of those supporting my life and work. My children, Sean, Brian, Tom, and Erin, and my daughters-in-law, Johann, Gail, and Angie, are my cheerleading squad, interpreters of the modern world, and most serious critics, who say, "We love you, Mom—let us save you from saying the wrong thing!" And finally, love and thanks to my partner, Marc, whose support, administrative skills, and presence keep me going when the going gets rough.

We're done!

Carol Garhart Mooney
Barnstead, New Hampshire
2009

Introduction

Social science doesn't exist in a vacuum. It doesn't spring from an absolute universe of "pure" inquiry and observation. Instead it tends to hew closely to social anxieties— what Kagan calls "historical nodes of worry." And these nodes of worry determine not only what social scientists study, but often enough, what results they find (because of the way their research is focused) and also, afterward, which of their findings are picked up by the media, and which ideas take hold and become popular with the public at large.

—Judith Warner, 2005

Perhaps there is no subject that so perfectly qualifies for Jerome Kagan's notion of "historical nodes of worry" as attachment theory (Kagan 1998). Often couched in articles about maternal employment, parent-infant bonding, or the effects of child care programs on infants, the topic of what is best for babies and who should decide is one the public never tires of. It has been almost constantly in the public eye for over twenty-five years. In her 2005 *New York Times* best seller, *Perfect Madness*, Judith Warner talks at great length about attachment theory. Initially this was not her intent. Warner, a journalist—not an educator or a researcher of human development—sought to answer the question, "Why are mothers so full of ambivalence?"

The question for Warner was both personal and perplexing. She spent her earliest years of "mothering" in France, where support structures and services that make the job feel less overwhelming are available to all new parents. In the United States, on the contrary, mothers seem to carry huge burdens of guilt, anxiety, and ambivalence. Warner claims it wasn't long after she returned to this country before she found herself caught up in the same spin of emotions. She set out to determine what this was all about. Her questions and answers became *Perfect Madness: Motherhood in the Age*

1

of Anxiety. Her question, "Why are mothers so full of ambivalence?" definitely caught the interest and opinions of the general public. Maternal ambivalence is common in the news. Titles such as "Who's Watching the Babies?" "The Mommy Wars," or "Mother's Dilemma: How Many Hours Away?" in the popular press always draw readers. People are interested in who is raising the children, how it should be accomplished, what the barriers are to doing it successfully, how the responsibility to the next generation should be fulfilled, who should be doing the care, and who should be paying for it. Separation and attachment persist in being newsworthy.

When I went to the bookstore to get a copy of Warner's book, the young woman at the counter said, "I can never remember if that's in Women's Studies or Child and Family." After reading the book, I understood her confusion. Maternal ambivalence certainly affects children and families, yet for many people, it remains a woman's issue. This is, perhaps, because women are the ones who give birth and are, in most cases, the primary caregivers during the first days and weeks of life.

Attachment is a delicate issue. Over the years, much has been written about attachment, bonding, separation and stranger anxiety, primary caregivers, effects of child care on infants, and the impact on infant development of all of the above. Some of the research is dated. Sometimes the terms are confused with each other. Often information is put in print that can only add to the ambivalence and guilt with which many parents struggle during their child's earliest weeks and months. Those of us doing the research should be asking ourselves, What is our responsibility? How much do we say, in full knowledge of parental anxiety, if we have no solutions to offer? Will infants be affected as adversely by their parents' anxiety over work schedules and long absences as they will be by the absence itself? Is it our responsibility to discover infants' needs, separated from the context of their families, neighborhoods, and government policies? How do we present our findings—and to whom?

Perhaps the best example of the confusion we all feel when approaching the study of attachment theory and infant caregiving is the work of Jay Belsky. His infant care research in 1985 calmed the anxieties of employed parents by finding no significant differences in development between home-reared infants and infants in quality child care, and then, a decade later, raised them again by sharing information about the behavioral effects of long hours, at an early age, in other than family care. Belsky's change of perspective was newsworthy.

Belsky originally stated that studies of infants reared in quality child care showed no differences between those children and their parent-reared cohorts. The problem, of course, is that few parents are aware of the poor quality of child care that is the norm in the United States. As child care professionals, we flinch when the media splashes anti–child care sound bites at already struggling young families. Yet our own industry knows that true quality care is in short supply. The national supply of quality infant care is deplorable. Yet we also know that we need to be more flexible than we once were in our definitions of what constitutes quality care. It is fair to say that there are many variables affecting quality and that families have different preferences and priorities when they choose care for their babies. Most of this information was missing from the press coverage of Belsky's original research findings. The press heralded his findings as good news for working parents—which it was.

But the rest of the story had yet to unfold. A decade later, when Belsky courageously shared a more cautious perspective, warning signs had led early childhood educators to question the long hours in non–family care for very young babies. Again the press had much to say about the situation; newspapers and magazines carried articles with titles like "Day Care Dilemma . . . What to Do?" and "New Findings Send Working Moms Back Home!" As we entered the new century, such discussions were presented in more detail. The story, however, remained pretty much the same for America's working parents.

It's the same story Selma Fraiberg shared many years ago in *Every Child's Birthright* (1977): children tend to do just fine in quality infant care. But how does a parent or even an infant care provider know what constitutes quality? For a while, we were pretty sure we knew what quality care was. Later we realized we hadn't taken enough time to determine the impact of variables such as ethnicity, parents' education levels, poverty, illness, individual temperament, and social mores on the actual quality of care. But even in the seventies, when practitioners in this country thought we were closer to the answers, research indicated that not nearly enough quality care was available. So do we acknowledge the very well-documented information that infants thrive in quality care—without mentioning the rest of the story?

An in-depth study of attachment theory shows us that, as Robert Karen points out, "The resistance to seeing the pain of deprived, neglected, or abused children has a long history" (1998, 22). This is not to say that children today who spend long hours in care are abused or neglected. Nevertheless, there is reason to believe that many unanswered questions contribute to general parental ambivalence and confusion about what is best for their young infants. It is difficult as parents and caregivers to acknowledge what Karen refers to as the "unwanted inheritance" we all bring to our family or professional work with infants and young children. That is the premise that the conditions of our own infancy affect how we view the total situation. This unwanted inheritance is not always conscious but is usually at play when parents struggle with work, child care schedules, and feelings about leaving their brand-new babies in the care of others. As both parents and professionals, we ask ourselves, "How much is too much when it comes to early separations between infants and their significant adults?"

To ponder solutions to these questions of parenthood and separations, we need to think first about our lack of preparation for such an important job. We live in a country where we require all high school graduates to take classes in government because they are future voters. I have no research data to back up my gut feeling that more high school graduates end up having children than end up voting. I know it feels wrong that graduating seniors are not required to look at life-span development (the study of how humans grow and change over a lifetime) and seriously consider what we know about marriage, family life, and child growth and development.

ABC's *Good Morning America* interviewed Jo Frost of the hit show *Supernanny* in 2008. She was asked if there was one prominent challenge she consistently encountered among young parents as they struggled in their parental roles. Frost responded immediately, "Parents want to know what is best for their kids, how to do it, and how to live with themselves when they know they've missed the mark." Parents and caregivers want to feel and be confident and competent when they approach their days with children. It is common for them to feel incompetent and lacking in confidence.

It doesn't have to be this way. Other countries (France, Israel, Japan, the Netherlands, to name a few) back up young families because doing so is best for the life of their nation. National policies in these countries are based on the premise (found only on bumper stickers in the United States) that "it takes a village to raise a child."

It is my hope to add a voice to the discussion. As in my previous work *Theories of Childhood*, I attempt to bring the thoughts, theories, and research of prominent minds to bear on our everyday work with children and their families. Before providing the background information on the theories of attachment, I'd like to offer the reader an idea of what to expect from this book.

It is not my intent to be comprehensive and scholarly. Instead, I'll attempt to share small bites of some of the major pieces in the debate surrounding attachment theory and its impact on parenting and infant caregiving. References will be included to assist those seeking more in-depth knowledge of the subject. This text is intended to familiarize the novice with some of the issues at play.

After providing a variety of definitions on the theory, I'll share information (historic and contemporary) on the primary threads of the story, from the work of John Bowlby to today's headlines on working families and their struggles to know what is best for their young children.

Following this introduction, I will provide a more thorough discussion of the lives and works of some of the founding attachment theorists: John Bowlby, Mary Ainsworth, Magda Gerber, John Kennell and Marshall Klaus, and T. Berry Brazelton.

The second part outlines the many areas of impact for parents and providers of infant care that attachment theory calls us to examine. Included are bonding, infant care, feeding practices, separation anxiety, stranger anxiety, responses to infant crying, and finally, parental or provider confidence and its impact on babies.

Defining Attachment

In his comprehensive study, *Becoming Attached*, Robert Karen acknowledges that the name John Bowlby is considered synonymous with attachment theory by many writers. Karen quotes

Bowlby's often-invoked words, "It is in our first relationship, usually with our mother, that much of our future well-being is determined" (1998, 5). Bowlby advanced our understanding of human development by focusing the discussion for the first time on the relationships and emotional bonds that are critical to healthy development in infants. Contemporary attachment theorists call on us to move beyond Bowlby's notion that unsatisfactory attachment bonds doom a child's opportunities to find fulfilling life experiences.

I follow the current understanding of attachment theory in believing that we are still in the process of learning about how babies and families connect with one another and what happens when that connection is disrupted. It is important for all of us who work with babies and their families to be schooled in the historic journey of attachment theory. It is also essential that we understand that our journey has just begun. As practitioners, we must study the past, observe the present, and plan for the future to assure that babies born in the twenty-first century receive the best care we can provide, based on our past and present knowledge of their critical needs.

Jean Mercer's outstanding book *Understanding Attachment: Parenting, Child Care, and Emotional Development* reminds us that Bowlby's work provides the foundation for studies of attachment but stresses that today's understanding of child development indicates "separation alone does not play as important a role in emotional development as Bowlby thought" (2006). It is our task to respond to new understandings of attachment and to propose further solutions for providing a strength-based understanding of how best to meet the needs of all babies and their families.

What do we mean when we talk about attachment in babies? The word *attachment* itself has several meanings. Even in professional discussion, it is often loosely substituted for bonding, relationships, or affection. Each of these can be considered a component of attachment, but for the purposes of this book, clarity of definition is essential.

Some of my preferred textbook definitions of *attachment* include:

- An enduring social tie of a child to a specific person, such as a mother or father (Mosher, Glover, Bruning 1987)

- An enduring emotional connection between people that produces a desire for continual contact as well as feelings of distress during separation (Berger 2001)

- A strong emotional bond between a baby or young child and a caring adult who is part of the child's everyday life—the child's attachment figure (Honig 2002)

Here are some traditional definitions framed by John Bowlby and Mary Ainsworth, two of the earliest theorists to study attachment:

- An affectional tie that one person or animal forms between himself and another specific one—a tie that binds them together in space and endures over time (Ainsworth 1967)

- "The dimension of the infant-caregiver relationship involving protection and security regulation. Within this theoretic framework, attachment is conceptualized as an intense and enduring affectional bond that the infant develops with the mother figure, a bond that is biologically rooted in the function of protection from danger" (Bowlby 1982).

If we look at all of these definitions of attachment theory, we can pull out some consistently used words. *Enduring* is one that predominates in both traditional and contemporary definitions. *Enduring* is a good place to begin. Everyone agrees that the effects of early relationships stay with us throughout our lifetime. Contemporary theories (Kagan 1998) caution us against the fatalistic view that poor early attachment triggers serious and irreversible challenges for children. Yet all agree that our earliest relationships tend to stay with us. Traditional definitions usually describe the mother-infant relationship, while later works use the words *mother, father,* or *significant adult*. One of the exciting changes to the discussion of infants, working parents, and attachment is that today it seems to include parents *and* other significant adults in a new baby's life. It is safe to say that although many variables affect lifespan development, babies' first relationships are among the most important, and attachment is the reason for this.

The study of attachment theory has increasingly regained the interest of American parents, providers, and infant teachers in the past two decades as the number of parents who return to employment immediately after their child's birth has increased. Our questions are many: What is the best age for babies to enter group care? Does it make a difference how many hours a day an infant is in out-of-home care? What is the best approach for supporting babies and their parents while they make this painful transition? What is the impact of provider turnover on very young children? How much preparation are teachers receiving in college programs to attentively meet the needs of infants and their parents? Are teachers being educated to treat infant care as systemic—that is, within the context of family and culture? These questions offer just a few of the reasons for parents and practitioners to look at attachment theory. It is my hope that this practical volume will familiarize you with some of the basic literature on attachment, help you ponder the many issues affected by our understanding of attachment, and give you the motivation to explore with families and colleagues the ways we can all work together to provide the best possible outcomes for all babies while we learn how best to meet their varied needs.

Historic Perspectives

Those whose work has focused on attachment theory have often been misunderstood, criticized, and rejected by colleagues. Sometimes too much emphasis has been placed on one area of research while other significant areas are neglected. As a group of researchers, attachment theorists have contributed greatly to the general knowledge of psychology, sociology, and medical science. They have passionately asserted that infants need an enduring relationship with significant, caring adults who come to know them well. Each year we learn more about the complexity of human beings and their developmental patterns. We can thank the attachment theorists for focusing our attention on the relational and social aspects of human development that we now know are tied to significant people in an infant's life, not merely to hunger or comfort.

The impetus for early attachment studies came from observing institutionalized infants. Several studies were conducted with this population. Many made reference to the sterile conditions, the single goal of meeting physical needs, and the absence of relationships with caregivers. One of the early works on life for institutionalized babies was René Spitz's sobering film, *Grief—A Peril in Infancy* (1947). Spitz documented the sadness and isolation of infants in institutional care and catalyzed the movement to determine the effects of maternal deprivation on new babies. Spitz went on to publish and lecture on this topic for many years. His work was hotly criticized, largely because it made people uncomfortable. His film was an exposé of the risks to unattached infants, yet it offered no plan to remedy the situation.

The response of many analysts to Spitz's film echoed Karen's statement about the long history of not wanting to look too closely at the pain of tiny babies separated from their families for many hours. Karen reports that a prominent New York analyst responded to Spitz's film by saying, "How could you do this to us?" (1998, 25). It is easy to think of young parents today responding to news flashes on "dangers of day care" with exactly the same words. It is heart wrenching to look at the tragedy of young, helpless infants and children. Sometimes we do want to look away.

(Weeks after writing the above paragraphs, I attended a New Hampshire/Vermont Association for the Education of Young Children [NH/VT AEYC] Administrators Conference where *Grief—A Peril in Infancy* was viewed as part of a seminar. Before the film had played for twenty minutes, attendees requested that the presenter move on with her session because the film was "too painful to watch.")

Many people in the United States believe children are best cared for in their own homes by family members. When providers of care to young infants are ambivalent about their work because they believe babies should be with their mothers in their early years, they find it difficult to provide optimal support to babies and their families. In 1977, Rita Warren referred to this dilemma as *child saving* and called it the number one occupational hazard for people who care for other people's children (Warren 1977, 8). Later, Janet Gonzalez-Mena echoed this notion, calling providers' attitude a *savior complex* in which they view themselves as saving children from their parents. Such attitudes can be redirected if teacher training programs spend time with students exploring the ways they can support rather than judge families.

When René Spitz filmed institutionalized babies, he hoped to raise the interest of those in the psychoanalytic community to the

tragedy of not investigating parent-infant separation. The seeds
sown by Spitz's work were fertilized by the young John Bowlby.
Bowlby began his career in the study of medicine but was quickly
drawn to what later would become the field of developmental
psychology. He volunteered at schools where children with adjustment and behavioral struggles were living. Bowlby had a hunch
that the detached nature of some of the children he worked with
was connected to early separation from family members. Following
this hunch became Bowlby's life work. Because the psychoanalytic
tradition in the early twentieth century focused on interpretation of
children's fantasy life, Bowlby's field observations were rejected by
his colleagues and largely considered irrelevant by the psychoanalytic community. This did not deter his interest or passion in discov-
ering the connection between behavior and early separation issues.
John Bowlby brought the issue of attachment to the forefront of
study for those interested in the causes and effects of early attachments on human behavior.

In the 1950s, Bowlby hired Mary Ainsworth to work with him
on his research studies. Ainsworth was a brilliant and exacting
researcher who was, like Bowlby, fascinated by babies, attachment,
and separation. She is best known to the early childhood community for developing her Strange Situation assessment. Like Bowlby,
she has often been criticized and ignored by the psychoanalytic
community. Attachment theory and the lifetime effects of early relationships between babies and their primary caregivers were her life
work. Sadly, she is often completely ignored by theorists writing
about significant issues in infants' first year of life.

Contemporary Perspectives

I focus here on the primary theorists whose work shaped our current approach to attachment and infant care. In addition to these
significant contributors, many contemporary researchers have
shaped our practices today. Some of these will be briefly high-
lighted here.

Tension has always existed between those who believe
that growth and development depend on heredity (nature) and
those who believe in the primacy of the environment (nurture).
In the early twentieth century, one area in which psychologists

(representing the nature half of the debate) and sociologists (representing the nurture half of the debate) agreed was the premise that babies loved their mothers because mothers were the source of sucking and hunger satisfaction. Usually at odds with each other's perspective, both agreed that mothers nurtured these natural needs, and that feeding and sucking were the primary force behind an infant's bond to the mother.

Bowlby, Spitz, and Ainsworth began discussions on the impact of relational factors as important parts of healthy development. Their work was furthered in 1958 by that of the psychologist Harry Harlow, now famous for his study of rhesus monkeys. Harlow questioned the psychoanalytic community's long-held belief that the reason babies loved their mothers was connected to feeding (1958). (I explain his experiments involving infant monkeys and their mothers in chapter 1.) Harlow's work opened the door to considering relationships in the early months and years of life.

Feeding practices, bonding, rooming in, and other attachment-related issues became hotly debated in professional circles and neighborhood parent groups as researchers, clinicians, and practitioners in the 1950s and 1960s spent more and more time focusing on the importance of early relationships. Contributions of people like John Kennell and Marshall Klaus in the United States and Dr. Frédérick Leboyer in France had powerful and positive effects on changes in birthing practices.

In the United States at the time, many practices in childbirth and infant care prioritized efficiency over the best interests of infants and families. New mothers were urged to bottle-feed their infants. Marketers went so far as to promote stuffed toy bottle props to free mothers from hours of holding and feeding their new infants. Automated swings and audio cassettes of lullabies were offered to replace long hours of rocking and singing. These "improvements" may have allowed the new parents to know the exact per ounce intake at a feeding, and the swings were definitely a blessing for busy moms who could not manage older children and a crying infant at the same time. However, these ideas did nothing to promote positive outcomes for babies. The renewed energy and focus on supportive practices for families and babies of the 1970s were an overdue improvement.

Dr. Benjamin Spock is remembered for offering advice to generations of young parents. He observed changes in research and practice and adapted to new ways of thinking when new information became available. His classic *Baby and Child Care* was the only baby book offering new parents advice during the 1950s and 1960s. Spock is to be admired for bringing parents new information that reversed some of his earlier advice. For example, in the third edition of *Baby and Child Care*, he cited research and current knowledge to support picking up a crying infant in the early weeks and months of life after suggesting in earlier editions that the baby be left to "cry it out."

Frédérick Leboyer was another voice in the 1970s to discuss the importance of the birth process for families. His *Birth without Violence* (1995) outlines an approach to childbirth that Leboyer had implemented during hundreds of deliveries in France. He spoke up about the fluorescent-lit, sterile delivery rooms in hospitals that he believed dehumanized the birth experience. Parents selecting his method of delivery could choose soft music, dim lights, and fresh air to welcome their infant to the world. Some families chose for the baby to be born underwater, allowing for a more gradual transition from the womb. Typically fathers or attending relatives would cut the cord, and infants went straight to the mother's breast rather than to the nursery for height, weight, and other traditional tests. Although the popularity of giving birth underwater was short lived, in the United States, its impact changed policies in hospitals around the country.

In 1976, John Kennell and Marshall Klaus published a small volume, *Maternal-Infant Bonding,* which addressed the impact of early separation or loss on family development. The authors made their case for a particular window of opportunity for parents and infants to develop a bond. They considered this time frame a critical period with the power to direct the future relationship between parent and infant as well as the infant's future relationships with others. Their research was cross-cultural and sought to determine what factors enhanced or decreased optimal conditions for making childbirth humane for all involved. The impact of their work has been felt across the United States in hospitals whose policies had excluded partners from the delivery room and prevented older siblings access to their mothers throughout a hospital stay; today, most hospitals have started opening the doors to families.

While many positive outcomes have been affected by the push for more humane birthing, negative consequences remain for families unable to participate in some of these positive changes. The zeal with which practitioners and the general public embraced the new approaches to giving birth was sometimes extreme. I remember a student sharing her story of giving birth by Caesarian section and having several women in her Lamaze class tell her a C-section was outrageous and that she had not truly "given birth." Similarly, parents whose children were rushed to larger hospitals for emergency care immediately after birth often experienced fear that they had not bonded with their child during the critical period. (These scenarios will be discussed at more length in chapter 2.) As the medical community experimented with more family-friendly policies and researchers continued to observe and study the first days and weeks of life, a greater sense of balance replaced some of the earlier zeal. In retrospect, we see that some of the theories were clearly overstated or not adequately founded. Nevertheless, the energy put into refining birthing processes, making them more sensitive to infant and family needs, has enhanced the birth experience in the United States for most families.

Magda Gerber is not as well-known to the general public as some of the other attachment theorists. Like the others, she devoted herself to developing policies in early care and education that supported infants and parents. She may be considered by some readers who are interested in early infancy as unlikely company for the other theorists included in the text. Her criteria differ from many contemporary policies and practices. She believed adults in Western countries had become too interested in doing everything to or for a baby rather than allowing the baby the personal freedom to find her own way (2003). She disliked commercial products that limited mobility or inquiry. She shared with other theorists a passionate desire to encourage practices that were supportive of children and families. Her lively and unique contributions give us all much to think about. Since a major theme of my book is developing tolerance for ambivalence and looking at the many ways of achieving the same goals, I believe including her work here has merit. Gerber believed in a different approach to achieving certain ends and would challenge us to question certain things we have been encouraged to take for granted.

Perhaps the most widely recognized parent-infant advocate in this country is pediatrician T. Berry Brazelton. He is a prolific writer whose work on families is appreciated by all those who take a serious interest in the rearing of the next generation. His interest in understanding the complexities of parent-child interaction and child growth and development is matched by his easy way of sharing significant information. Brazelton is a familiar face on Capitol Hill, where administrations for the past three decades have solicited his input on government policies for children and families. He sees his mission as fostering a sense of competence in parents that will lead to loving parenting. Brazelton has done much in his lifetime to ease the burdens and guilt of twentieth- and twenty-first century parents as they struggle with the demands of balancing family and work.

No discussion of attachment theory is complete without the voice of Harvard's Dr. Jerome Kagan. Kagan has long rejected some of attachment theory. He believes too much emphasis has been placed on the earliest days and weeks of life and that cross-cultural studies suggest children can thrive at later ages after difficult beginnings (1998). Like Brazelton, Kagan has spent his life studying the development of children from birth to adolescence. He has focused on temperament and environmental and genetic impacts on growing humans.

Attachment theory is complex, multifaceted, and ever changing. Kagan's repudiation of it does not lead us to ignore the theories on attachment that have grown and changed for decades. Kagan's work suggests that we proceed with caution, that we not overlook a child's ability to thrive even if her first relationship was not what we would like for all children. By studying the ideas and theories presented for the past several decades on parent-infant or infant-provider attachments, we can construct approaches to caregiving that support the needs of babies, parents, and providers as they engage in what all can agree are significant relationships that have a huge impact on children's future success.

Part 1

Major Theorists,
Their Lives and Work

Chapter 1: John Bowlby

When a baby is born he cannot tell one person from another and indeed can hardly tell person from thing. Yet, by his first birthday he is likely to have become a connoisseur of people. Not only does he come quickly to distinguish familiars from strangers but amongst his familiars he chooses one or more favorites. They are greeted with delight; they are followed when they depart; and they are sought when absent. Their loss causes anxiety and distress; their recovery, relief and a sense of security. On this foundation, it seems, the rest of his emotional life is built—without this foundation there is risk for his future happiness and health.

—John Bowlby (1967)

John Bowlby was born in London in 1907. He was the fourth of six children in a traditional, upper-middle-class English family. As was the fashion for his class and time, Bowlby and his siblings were raised by nannies and had very little contact with their parents. Middle-class women at the time believed parental attention and affection resulted in lack of discipline. Children typically spent an hour a day at tea time with their mother. Bowlby had one nanny to whom he was quite attached. She left the family's employ when he was four years old. As an adult, Bowlby described this loss as similar to the loss of a mother. At seven, again typical for his social class, he was sent to boarding school. He remembered this as a terrible time in his life. Bowlby's lifework focused on the effects of early separation and loss on life-span development. It has been said that his own childhood experiences drove his professional interest and gave him tremendous sensitivity to the suffering of young children.

Bowlby's father was a surgeon. He directed John to medical school. Bowlby was an excellent student and won prizes for outstanding intellectual achievement. He began his career at Trinity College, Cambridge. He took time after college to volunteer for children with serious emotional and behavioral challenges. From the beginning, Bowlby was interested in the connections between family life and children's mental health and behavior. Though this connection is commonplace to the study of child growth and development today, it was uncommon at the time.

A friend urged Bowlby to change the direction of his study from medicine to psychology. While still in medical school, he enrolled in the Institute for Psychoanalysis. Though qualified in both medicine and psychoanalysis, Bowlby's sustained interest was in the mental and emotional health of children. From his earliest studies, Bowlby was convinced that deviant or troubled behaviors in late childhood and adolescence had their origins in the family system. He believed the first relationships in infancy set the tone for all later love relationships. He believed that disruption to these first relationships or poor quality in these relationships accounted for trauma and troubling behaviors in adolescence and adult life.

His ideas were not well received in the psychoanalytic community. The prevailing thought at the time was that one needed to look inside the mind at dreams and fantasies to determine the source of neuroses or deviant behaviors. The analysis of troubled individuals was the foundation of psychoanalytic studies. Bowlby believed that observation would yield more information about an individual's reality. He believed the troubled youth he worked with experienced problems because of external causes rooted in their homes and in the earliest experiences that had occurred there or, conversely, in the situations that ideally should have occurred there but did not.

Bowlby's first professional papers presented the idea that two environmental factors early in life can introduce lifetime challenges for individuals. The first of these, which received much negative attention in his early career, is that separation from or the death of a mother results in lifelong struggles for the individual. The second, which today seems like an ordinary idea, is that the emotional attitude of a parent toward a child has life-shaping effects.

Bowlby proposed that often the attitude of a parent toward a child is deeply affected by unresolved issues from his or her own childhood. Today these ideas are accepted as commonplace by psychologists, educators, and sociologists and are part of the well-known foundations of development. When Bowlby first presented his ideas, they were not taken seriously by academicians in any discipline.

At the time, analysts tended to focus on problems around feeding, toileting, or exposure to parents' sexual intercourse. All of these issues and their interpretations tended to flow from Freud's theory and practice of psychoanalysis. So when Bowlby suggested that observations of parental behaviors in the home might provide a clue to a child's development, he was largely dismissed by the psychoanalytic community. At the time, analysts did not consider it part of their task to give any consideration at all to the real experiences of patients. "Almost by definition it was assumed that anyone interested in the external world could not be interested in the internal world, indeed was almost certainly running away from it" (Karen 1998, 38).

Bowlby was somewhat single-minded in his approach to his work. The fact that few found his work as fascinating as he did was not discouraging to him. He was certain he had discovered a key to unlocking the mysteries of deviant human behavior and distress. He spent his life trying to understand the effects of early relationships on mental health and stability in adulthood. It has often been said of Bowlby that he was shy and distant and that these characteristics, as well as his interest in early childhood, were based on his own unhappy childhood. Bowlby had tremendous insight into the lives of children. In his later years, he spoke passionately about the ways society should respond to the needs of young children. His criticism of patterns of child rearing that were isolating or harsh could be viewed as his indictment of his own childhood.

Throughout his career, Bowlby struggled with the fact that his fellow psychoanalysts did not acknowledge his findings. He was unable to provide a scientific explanation for what he knew to be true from his observations of children and families. His goals for establishing a more sensitive model of developmental psychology were challenged by the psychoanalytic community while he was researching attachment and loss. Bowlby felt certain his understanding was key to a more progressive model, but at the time, nearly all research was quantitative. Today qualitative research studies are met with respect that did not exist in Bowlby's time. The dilemma was in rating such qualities as abusiveness, unkindness, and mistreatment, even when these were acknowledged by the psychoanalytic community. Bowlby was sure that, beyond actual abuse or cruelty, unresponsive or manipulative parenting styles contributed to later mental health problems in individuals.

It was for these reasons that Bowlby is best known for his studies and theories of attachment based on early parent-child separation. It was not that attachment theory captured his interest more than other broad areas of early development, but parent-child separation could be easily documented and was less open to interpretation or misunderstanding than, for example, determining what constitutes unresponsive maternal behavior.

His interests were far-reaching and seem surprisingly contemporary. For example, the Perry Preschool Project has captured the interest of contemporary politicians and the media for its emphasis on addressing the problems of our youngest citizens before they are in need of remedial services or juvenile interventions because of crimes committed. Half a century ago, Bowlby advocated early intervention and worked tirelessly to change national policies in support of young children and their families.

Bowlby's work with troubled youths led him to believe that the critical questions to be asked are: What conditions in a child's rearing lead to stability and strength rather than deviance? How can we nurture such strengths? How can we help young children see that everyone has positive and negative thoughts and feelings about the people we love? How do we give serious attention to the costs of early separation from family? What policies can be put in place to avert these situations? Bowlby fought to send the message that policies needed changing.

Bowlby was sure that, beyond actual abuse or cruelty, unresponsive or manipulative parenting styles contributed to later mental health problems in individuals.

For example, Bowlby believed that families, especially poor families, needed greater assistance. He thought that more people should be trained professionally in marriage and child guidance and in work with parents of the very young. He wanted the public to understand that the funds required to put supportive programs in place would be far less than the later costs of institutional care and delinquency (1951).

Bowlby has often been accused of being too hard on mothers, but much of this impression has come from words taken out of context or popularized by his opponents. He was actually a man of great empathy for motherhood. He knew mothering was the hardest and least appreciated job to be done, and he often criticized government and social agencies for not being more appreciative of or proactive in supporting young parents. He observed that comments about parenthood were often made glibly by those who had not experienced it and that people should be more cautious with their indictments.

Bowlby was sympathetic to the ordinary plight of children raised in an era in which adults gave little attention to the pressing needs and fears of children. He was a proponent of progressive education and believed that children needed attention, affection, and freedom to develop optimally (1940). None of these interests has become as much a part of Bowlby's legacy as his work on maternal deprivation.

Post–World War II England provided optimal conditions for Bowlby's work. Orphanages were full of infants abandoned or orphaned during the war. In addition to the film René Spitz was making on institutionalized infants, Harry Harlow's work at the University of Wisconsin gave the scientific community reason to reevaluate its position on nourishment as the basis for an infant's attachment to its mother. In Harlow's studies, rhesus monkeys were deprived of their mothers and then given either a terry cloth mother or a wire one. Harlow's studies dealt the first scientific blow to the belief that affectional ties were based on nursing: for rhesus monkeys, at least, cuddly contact proved far more important to attachment and survival (1958), an observation that brought great joy to the Bowlby camp. The fact that monkeys exposed to terry cloth mothers survived at a higher rate than those whose wire mothers offered nourishment but no comfort was a huge step forward for those engaged in attachment studies. (Later studies with the rhesus monkeys indicated that the early separation from biological parents left these monkeys vulnerable to poor peer relationships and diminished ability to raise their young.) There was no doubt that Harlow's studies confirmed the work of Bowlby and others who stated the case for relationships as significant to emotional health. Harlow proved that comfort is a need of the very young as well as a factor in infant feeding. Bowlby was grateful for Harlow's contributions to the discussion of attachment behaviors. The two men followed each other's work for years. "Together they were able to intertwine biology and psychology in a way previously unimagined" (Karen 1998).

Current understanding of growth and development and psychology forces us to acknowledge that Bowlby's work overstates the necessity of mother-child attachment. As part of his Ecological Systems Theory, Urie Bronfenbrenner stresses the importance of chronology to our study of growth and development (1979). Each historical era and its attending sociological conditions shape any body of research as well as the public's reaction to it. In *Understanding Attachment*, Jean Mercer echoes this concept in relation to research generally and Bowlby's work specifically. "Most theories develop gradually," she asserts, "but there comes a moment when they coalesce and are presented to the world in a nearly complete form. Bowlby's attachment theory reached this stage in the late 1950s, and it was published in several important papers. These papers drew together Bowlby's ideas about the reasons for children's emotional attachments to their mothers and caregivers, about the observable behaviors that indicate attachment and about the consequences of separation from a familiar attachment figure. Although Bowlby's ideas became further elaborated over the years, these papers are the true foundation of modern attachment theory" (2006, 37).

Most contemporary theorists assume that what does and doesn't happen during the earliest stages of life affect development for a lifetime in powerful ways. Unmet needs in infancy continue to haunt us until they are eventually reconciled. This assumption is called *infant determinism*. Jean Mercer points out that we rarely question this premise, even though the evidence to support it is not conclusive. She suggests that not enough research has been done to identify the ways in which later social experiences and relationships also affect adult development (2006). The work of Erik Erikson encouraged developmental theorists to believe that significant needs for love and trust continue to be present in life's challenges. Erikson proposes that opportunities to resolve these unmet needs surface again and again until one is able to adequately meet one's needs for love and trust (1968).

Harvard's Jerome Kagan goes so far as to identify infant determinism as a "seductive idea" that should be approached with caution. His assessment of Bowlby's attachment theory is possibly best understood through Bronfenbrenner's view of chronology and its effect on all that happens in human development. According to Kagan, "The swell of enthusiasm for attachment theory was also, in part, an understandable reaction to the excessive cruelties of the Second World War. The atrocities generated a desire among psychologists and psychiatrists for a conception of human nature with less dark, Freudian pessimism. Erik Erikson's creative intuition to replace Freud's oral stage with a stage of trust satisfied this hunger for a more humane, less selfish infant who was receptive to parental love" (1998, 94).

Kagan believes that Bowlby "sensed that the angst of his historical era was a rupture of family and social bonds, and he guessed that a child's secure attachment to a parent protected her from fear and inoculated her against future uneasiness." Kagan writes that in previous centuries "parents wanted their children to be able to cope with adversity, but they thought forcing their children to cope with difficulty was a better preparation for life than showering them with love and protecting them from worry" (1998, 95).

I will discuss Kagan's ideas further when I look at contemporary influences on our current notion of attachment theory and its place in the broader context of human development. In concluding discussion of Bowlby's theory of attachment, however, it is important for me to note that scientific study of human development includes looking at how things change and how they remain the same.

There is no doubt that John Bowlby, the father of attachment theory, contributed enormously to our understanding of the human condition. It is important for us to take his theories and test them against contemporary observations in early childhood development and education. We must also acknowledge his work as the foundation for all of us who study children and families and who view emotional connections as critical to healthy human development and success in adult life.

Suggestions for Further Reading

Bowlby, John. 1970. *Child care and the growth of love.* 2nd ed. Baltimore: Penguin.

Bowlby, John. 1951. *Maternal care and mental health.* Geneva: World Health Organization.

Bowlby, John. 1982, 1980, 1973. *Attachment and loss.* (Vols. 1, 2, & 3) New York: Basic.

*I did not intend this as a way of assessing
attachment, but it certainly wound up as
that. We began to realize that it fit in with
our impressions after seventy-two hours
of observation in an amazing way. But
instead of seventy-two hours of observation we could do a Strange Situation in
twenty minutes.*

—**Mary Ainsworth (from Karen 1998)**

Mary Ainsworth's description of her now-famous Strange Situation
gives us a peek at the no-nonsense woman who created it. Mary
Dinsworth Salter was born in Glendale, Ohio, in 1913. She was the
oldest of three daughters. Her parents were college educated and
provided a middle-class life for their family. The Salter girls enjoyed
a comfortable home life and many rich educational opportunities.
The family moved to Canada when Mary was five years old. Her
education, from a bachelor's degree through her doctorate, was
completed at the University of Toronto.

Though Ainsworth's childhood has been described as ideal,
there were troubling emotional currents in the home that led her
to feel her childhood had somehow failed her. Her own insecuri-
ties led her to passionately pursue a career that questioned how
secure attachment was formed. She studied theories on security as
the primary foundation of a healthy personality. When she took an
abnormal psychology course, she looked at the close relationship
between parents and children as a cornerstone to secure feelings
for young children. She shared thoughts on these pieces of her own
development in a series of interviews with Robert Karen that are
included in his book *Becoming Attached* (1998).

In 1950, Mary Salter married Leonard Ainsworth. She moved
with him to London, where he finished his graduate work and she
answered an advertisement in the *London Times* for a research

assistant. The ad had been placed by John Bowlby. Answering that ad proved to have an enormous impact on the direction her life-work would take, as it did on John Bowlby's work.

Bowlby recognized at once that Ainsworth had a brilliant mind and a passion for research. He was excited that her education, interests, and early research were much like his own. Like Bowlby, Ainsworth was convinced that observation of infants in their home environment contributed a more accurate way to assess emotional stability and attachments than focusing on the memories and dreams of insecure adults (1967). Thus, like Bowlby, her approach was contrary to the contemporary practice of the psychoanalytic community. In his initial interview with her, Bowlby saw that Ainsworth was an independent thinker who was experienced and intelligent enough to know what could be validated by empirical data and what could not. Both researchers struggled throughout their careers with the significance of empirical data. They trusted their gut responses and knew their observations in natural settings provided information as important as what could be quantified in a laboratory setting.

Like Bowlby, Ainsworth was convinced that observation of infants in their home environment contributed a more accurate way to assess emotional stability and attachments than focusing on the memories and dreams of insecure adults.

Like Bowlby, Ainsworth believed her research, and psychology in general, could be used to improve the human condition. So she moved forward with enthusiasm and conviction, even when others in the academic community judged her harshly. She worked with Bowlby for three and a half years, and their interest fed each other's work for the rest of their lives. This mutual interest and support was very much in evidence in 1961 when Bowlby asked Ainsworth to represent him at the World Health Organization. Robert Karen describes Ainsworth's efforts on Bowlby's behalf:

> *Ainsworth produced a brilliantly coherent statement of Bowlby's and her views. For the first time in one place she clarified many of the misunderstandings, success-fully repudiated oft-repeated criticisms, and smoothed out some of Bowlby's own apparent inconsistencies and*

dubious hunches. Ainsworth broke the debate down into its constituent parts. She noted that the catch-all phrase "maternal deprivation" was actually composed of three different dimensions—the lack of maternal care (insufficiency), distortion of maternal care (neglect or mistreatment), and discontinuity in maternal care (separations, or the child's being given one mother figure and then another)—and that these three dimensions were frequently confounded, making it difficult to study any one of them alone. Carefully sifting through dozens of studies, she assessed what they had to say about the effects of each of these conditions, and, in doing so, she was able to disentangle many apparent contradictions (1998, 123).

Bowlby had refined his work to focus on discontinuity of care. Like Ainsworth, he was interested in maternal deprivation but found it easier to apply scientific method to one aspect of maternal deprivation than to the other two dimensions Ainsworth had so clearly outlined for the World Health Organization. Ainsworth moved beyond maternal deprivation to study other aspects of infant development. She knew even as a student that she would one day focus on the relationships of infants and mothers during the first year of life.

In 1954, Mary Ainsworth followed her husband from London to Uganda, where he had accepted a teaching position. She secured a small grant from the East African Institute of Social Research. She spent a month with other researchers, learning the language and customs of the Ugandan people. With few resources but great enthusiasm, she began one of the earliest studies on infant development in the twentieth century.

When Ainsworth began her research, she still believed that attachment behavior in human infants was associated with the experience of feeding. But Ainsworth was an expert at observation. As she watched infants and mothers in their own home environments, she began to see the picture as much broader and deeper than theorists suggested. Her style was different from the laboratory research then being done in Europe and the United States. She approached the women in Uganda as an outsider who was interested in learning from and about them. She also presented herself as a friend and helper. She and her associates went into women's homes at regular intervals and did whatever needed to be done to support and help these parents. She got to know them. She got to know their infants. She began developing lists of behaviors that she believed were an indication of an attachment between mothers and their babies.

As her lists developed, they included behaviors like these:

- crying when the mother leaves

- following the mother

- showing concern for the mother's whereabouts

- scrambling over the mother

- burying the face in the mother's lap

- using the mother as a safe haven when in a strange situation

- flying to the mother when frightened

- greeting her through smiling, crowing, clapping, lifting the arms, and general excitement

(1967)

Ainsworth noticed that once babies were able to crawl and walk, they moved away from their mothers to explore their surroundings. If a surprising or different element entered their surroundings, these babies immediately headed back to their mothers. She observed this behavior in so many of the infants that it led her to hypothesize that babies use their mothers as a secure base to depart from and return to in their explorations of the world. Returning to her initial studies of security, she suggested that securely attached infants have the courage to leave their mothers and investigate their surroundings, knowing they can return to their mothers if they become anxious.

It also occurred to Ainsworth that a broad range of differences in development and style existed among babies and mothers as they worked on the development of relationships. She decided that a very complex set of circumstances contributed to the mother-child relationship. She saw many differences in development from child to child. She concluded that methods of care varied from culture to culture and affected these relationships as well. She noted that many anxious babies seemed to be the offspring of anxious mothers. She noticed that mothers separated from their husbands or families experienced more stress and seemed to pass it on to their infants (1967).

Ainsworth found it difficult to articulate clear lists of variables indicating secure and insecure attachment. She understood the complexity of her subject matter. She knew that determining precise variables was not easy when observing infants and mothers; multiple causes affected the outcomes.

Ainsworth found that mothers who gave the most care to their young had infants who were securely attached, while mothers who were not present for their infants had babies who were less securely attached. She was quick to realize that there were exceptions to these observations. Were then quantity and quality of care the same thing? Ainsworth thought not. She believed something about the quality of the care must be an important factor, but she could not prove this. As a fastidious researcher, Ainsworth struggled to make sense of all the information she had collected. Her book *Infancy in Uganda* was not published until 1967, long after studies in Uganda were behind her.

In 1956, Mary Ainsworth once again moved to accompany her husband, this time to a new job in the United States. Mary soon found a position at Johns Hopkins University in Baltimore. She taught courses on personality assessment but longed to replicate her study of infants and mothers in this country. It was many years before she was able to convince those at Johns Hopkins to fund her work. In 1963, she was awarded a grant, which was meager, but her interest in and passion for research were keen. Like her work in Uganda, Ainsworth's Baltimore research was conducted in what was still considered an unusual fashion. She and her colleagues did their observations in home settings. They hoped that by being friendly and helpful to the mothers in the study, they could assess mother-infant relationships more accurately. Although Ainsworth hoped to pick up her earlier study, in the years since she had conducted it, several other questions had surfaced. Ainsworth now wondered, for example, if attachment behaviors were universal. Would she see a different array of behaviors in America? Today, studying behavior in the context of culture is commonplace. In the early 1960s in Baltimore, Maryland, Mary Ainsworth was a pioneer of cultural research.

When Ainsworth compared the data from her Baltimore study to that from her Uganda study, she was delighted to observe that most of the attachment behaviors were the same. This made sense to her. She believed her attachment theory was tapping into a universal behavior. She believed that babies studied around the world would demonstrate similar behaviors when separated from their mothers. She wanted to pursue her idea of the mother as secure base. It was difficult to compare the Baltimore babies to the Uganda babies for this purpose. In Uganda, infants were used to always being with their mothers; if the mothers left the room, the babies would typically cry uncontrollably. In the United States, however, babies were used to their mothers entering and leaving the room more frequently. Ainsworth wondered how to test for the secure basis in a valid way. She decided that if she and her colleagues could not test for the "secure base" in Baltimore homes, they would set up a "strange situation" on the university campus. There they could observe the babies reacting to their mother's departures in a more stressful environment.

Ainsworth and her colleagues knew what they wanted to observe. They decided on a room filled with engaging toys. They would observe a baby as she explored this new space with her mother nearby. They would then introduce a stranger to the room to increase the stress level. They would check the infant's response. They would then have the baby left alone in the room with the stranger. They would observe the infant's behavior at separation and at reunion. In an interview with Robert Karen, Mary Ainsworth stated that it had taken only about a half hour for them to determine the process (Karen 1998).

The procedure was called the Strange Situation, and it has become a widely used, well-validated method of determining an infant's attachment behaviors to her caregivers. It is by far the most well-known piece of Ainsworth's work. The Strange Situation is included in most texts on infant development. It is briefly described as a twenty-minute observation of infant play in an unfamiliar room while both familiar and unfamiliar adults enter and leave the room. Its purpose is to determine a child's attachment behaviors, based on the usual comings and goings of significant adults as well as on documented responses to unfamiliar adults. The child's responses are observed and documented as the child experiences this sequence of events:

1. Parent and infant are introduced to the experimental room.

2. Parent and infant are alone. Parent does not participate while infant explores.

3. Stranger enters, converses with parent, then approaches infant. Parent leaves inconspicuously.

4. First separation episode: stranger's behavior is geared to that of infant.

5. First reunion episode: parent greets and comforts infant, then leaves again.

6. Second separation episode: infant is alone.

7. Continuation of second separation episode: stranger enters and gears behavior to that of infant.

8. Second reunion episode: parent enters, greets infant, and picks up infant. Stranger leaves inconspicuously.

Throughout this process, researchers observe two aspects of the child's behavior:

- The amount of exploration the child engages in throughout the process

- The child's reactions to the departure and return of the parent or primary caregiver

Results of the Strange Situation categorize infant behaviors into three forms of attachment behavior:

- Secure attachment

- Anxious-ambivalent insecure attachment

- Anxious-avoidant insecure attachment

(1984)

The child described as securely attached to an adult explores her surroundings with enthusiasm, checking back with her secure base (mother, father, or primary caregiver) periodically. During the Strange Situation, the securely attached infant engages with strangers if her mother is nearby, cries when her mother leaves the room, is happy to reunite with her mother when she returns, and does not engage with strangers if her mother is not nearby. The securely attached child tends to develop a sense of security that allows her to cope with problems and to adapt well to unfamiliar situations. Parents of securely attached infants tend to be responsive and sensitive to their infant's needs in an appropriate way. This style of attachment behavior is marked by both the positive, close relationship with the parent or caregiver and the infant's willingness to be independent in exploring her surroundings. This is the child who typifies the "secure base" theory. She snuggles happily with her caregiver, then wiggles down to check out the space and the toys or just to wander. She looks back to her caregiver to smile or simply to check on his continued presence. She returns now and again for encouragement or if a situation makes her feel uncomfortable. The securely attached child is both comfortable and confident.

The child assessed as anxious-ambivalent insecurely attached tends to express distress when near strangers or unfamiliar settings, whether the parent or caregiver is nearby or not. The child exhibits extreme anxiety and distress when the parent departs and yet, when the parent returns, is often resistant to reuniting. This style of attachment is confusing to researchers, parents, and providers. Some psychologists suggest that it is the result of inconsistent parenting styles. Ainsworth suggests that the parent responds to the child on her own schedule rather than that of the infant. Given the many demands on parents, it seems almost unfair to say they should always respond solely in terms of the infant's needs. It is difficult for both parents and infants when ambivalent attachment patterns set in.

The anxious-avoidant insecurely attached assessment is perhaps the most challenging of all attachment behaviors to understand and support. These infants show little behavior indicating interest in the adults in the room, regardless of what adults are present. They tend to avoid or ignore both parents and primary caregivers, whether there are strangers nearby or not. For these children, strangers are not treated much differently from parents or primary providers. They show little emotional response. Some of these babies react exactly the same whether they are in the room with parents, primary caregivers, or strangers, or they are alone. Infants assessed with anxious-avoidant insecure attachment react in a similar style to those studied in institutions by Bowlby and Spitz. They lack affect. These babies don't seem to believe they can affect their fate. They don't seem to believe that adults in their lives will respond to their signals of distress. These children come to believe that communication of their needs makes no difference at all.

In reviewing the three attachment styles outlined by Ainsworth and her colleagues, we can't help but ask certain questions. For instance, if a parent is emotionally unavailable to an infant's signals because of unemployment, substance abuse, or other real issues in the lives of young families, what happens if those circumstances improve? As practitioners, we need to remind parents and each other that circumstances for children and parents are constantly changing. For example, a child who is insecurely attached at age one may become securely attached by age two, and this would considerably brighten ideas about any long-term effects of insecure attachment. The idea that early relationships do not necessarily determine later social relationships is important. When we are more flexible in our views about attachment as a changing characteristic, we provide a stronger basis for intervention and family support.

The child described as securely attached to an adult explores her surroundings with enthusiasm, checking back with her secure base (mother, father, or primary caregiver) periodically.

As we think about attachment behaviors and their ability to change over time, we can thank Mary Ainsworth for first calling our attention to this very important part of human growth and development. Her contributions took Bowlby's initial work on infants to a more sophisticated level. Because she was rigorous in her pursuit of valid research, she not only contributed to our body of foundational infant research but also paved the way for others after her to emphasize the importance of direct observation. She earned the respect of her colleagues for her careful, direct observations while proving that observations of infants and mothers in their natural home environments could lead us to important research questions that might never have surfaced had the work not begun in comfortable home settings.

Ainsworth died in Charlottesville, Virginia, at the age of eighty-five, retired from the University of Virginia, but she had continued to be active in her work until the very end of her life. Kurt Vonnegut (1999) referred to her obituary in the *New York Times* as "extravagantly favorable." It stated that Mary Ainsworth had contributed more to our knowledge of infant-parent attachment than anyone else who had researched it. It noted that her reference to absentminded lack of bonding was also a significant contribution to the field.

Many students of growth and development are in tune with dramatic losses and interruptions that affect attachment. Ainsworth called our attention to the routine ways that the attachment relationship can be compromised if we are not mindful of its importance. Her research in London, Uganda, and the United States encouraged discussion about the need of infants for secure attachments. Although her belief that an individual will remain anxious if this first relationship goes awry is still hotly debated, without Ainsworth's input, the conversation would not be part of our continued search for the keys to emotional stability and comfort.

Suggestions for Further Reading

Ainsworth, Mary. 1967. *Infancy in Uganda: Infant care & the growth of love.* Baltimore: Johns Hopkins Press.

Mercer, Jean. 2006. *Understanding attachment.* Westport, CT: Praeger Publishers.

Viorst, Judith. 1998. *Necessary losses.* New York: Simon & Schuster.

Chapter 3: Magda Gerber

*I would like everyone who works with
infants to try less and enjoy it more.*

—Magda Gerber (Mangione 1988)

Magda Gerber was born in Budapest. The daughter of wealthy parents, she was urged to develop her full potential. Because she was a child of affluence, her parents provided nannies and tutors to assure her the best academic opportunities. She studied at the Sorbonne in Paris. Multilingual and passionate about her work, she did much to set the tone for quality infant care and parenting programs in the United States and around the world.

As was common during the time, she married very young. She was only eighteen when she married, and she had children soon thereafter. Gerber had nannies for her children, just as her mother had. One day, Gerber observed the nanny trying to force food upon her child, and this disturbed her deeply. She told the nanny to leave and surprised her husband when he returned from work by stating that she would take care of the children herself. When she began caring for the children, she was amazed to discover how important a job caring for an infant was. She continued to study and think about how to respond to her children.

It was an accident of time and circumstance that led Magda Gerber to her lifework. When her daughter, Erika, was in primary school, she came down with a sore throat while their pediatrician was away. The mother of Erika's school friend, Anna, was a pediatrician. Gerber called the friend's mother, Emmi Pikler, to check Erika's sore throat. The call changed her life. Gerber began to tell the doctor about her child's condition. Emmi Pikler shushed her and focused on the child. Respectfully, she asked the young child what hurt and how. Magda Gerber was amazed by two things: how cooperative her daughter was with a stranger when she was feeling so poorly, and how serious and respectful the pediatrician treated her young patient. Gerber later referred to this as her Aha! moment. She went back to school to get a master's degree in early childhood and was mentored by Emmi Pikler in her unusual approach to caring for young children.

Gerber joined Pikler at the National Methodological Institute (better known as Loczy, for the street it was located on) in 1945. Loczy was established by the Hungarian government to care for orphaned children whose mothers had died in childbirth. Gerber worked with Pikler until 1956, when the political situation in Hungary made it impossible for her to remain there. Reportedly, Gerber's husband and her young teenaged daughter were imprisoned for political reasons. (Gerber was very closemouthed about her personal history, so not much is known for sure.) Perhaps these events intensified the feelings Gerber had about personal freedom and allowing babies and all others to develop their personal independence (Weber 2003).

Magda Gerber and her family escaped from Hungary and eventually settled in California. There Gerber set about using the many lessons she had learned from her mentor, Emmi Pikler. Gerber worked with autistic children for several years and then founded the Demonstration Infant Project in Palo Alto, California, with Dr. Thomas Forrest to implement Pikler's techniques. At this project, Gerber focused on respect for infants and their own processes of development. She expanded on that work by adding a family component. Working with the parents of the infants, she eventually cofounded (with Dr. Forrest) Resources for Infant Educarers (RIE). It is this work that received the most attention from the early childhood community.

Gerber's interest in the first year of life led her to teach child development at UCLA and Pacific Oaks College. Her work has been included in professional journals and videos, such as *Respectfully Yours*, developed by the California State Department of Education and WestEd (Mangione 1988). Her training tools are used to educate infant teachers and Early Head Start teachers in the United States.

Her work has been picked up by the international community as well. The world continues to search for answers to the question, How shall we raise our children? Gerber's response is probably best summed up in the words *respect* and *authenticity*.

Gerber died in the spring of 2007. She is remembered for many things, including successfully adapting Dr. Pikler's work to be accepted in America. Nevertheless, Gerber's work went well beyond her association with Pikler. Magda Gerber's legacy is the contributions she made as a parent educator and teacher. Her students will work in RIE centers and other infant programs to rear the next generation.

It is interesting to me that when I have mentioned Magda Gerber as someone to include in my book on attachment, many colleagues have been surprised. Like most of the theorists included in this work, Gerber has sometimes been misunderstood. Her position stands apart from much of the modern rhetoric on what babies need. During the 1970s and '80s when the popular trend was to carry babies around at all times, Gerber suggested that wise parents might give their infant some opportunities to learn to amuse themselves. Unlike many who write about infancy, Gerber wrote not from the perspective of years of training and practice but with the humble honesty of a parent. She shares her surprise with us about how challenging the job can actually be. She acknowledges that families have many different comfort levels and that our job as infant care providers is to support families while they find their comfort levels. She is not arbitrary. She believes her way is *a* way, not *the* way.

Respect is the basis of the RIE philosophy. Gerber stands out as an educator for the way that respect is woven throughout every piece of helpful information she shares. She is not evangelical—which must be appreciated by young families. Many of the young parents attracted to theories like William and Martha Sears's *Attachment Parenting* (2001) acknowledge the tremendous pressure among those who follow attachment parenting to breast-feed, cosleep, and keep their baby with them at all times. These expectations make some families uncomfortable. We don't experience this discomfort when we read Magda Gerber.

In *Dear Parent: Caring for Infants with Respect* (2003), Gerber talks realistically about how hard life is in the first weeks with a new baby. She cautions new parents about total exhaustion and how unprepared most parents are for the effects of sleep deprivation. Gerber makes practical suggestions to young parents. She suggests that they slow down and focus on getting to know their baby.

She also makes suggestions for grandparents and friends about how to support the new family. A continuing theme in her work is time: she believes all parents and child care providers are too busy. She urges all of us to slow down.

Over the years, Gerber has presented many ways to help parents and babies form strong attachments. More than most parent educators, she urges parents to get rid of their guilt. Although her tone is respectful, she is skeptical of some of the modern theorists who suggest that babies and parents bond to each other by spending every waking (and even sleeping) hour together. She acknowledges that the baby should know her parents are nearby and will always be there for her, but she reminds parents that they needn't drop everything and run the minute they hear a whimper. One of her strengths is putting an idea out there for families with the suggestion that they mull it over and decide which pieces fit their way of parenting and which don't.

Respect is the basis of the RIE philosophy. Gerber stands out as an educator for the way that respect is woven throughout every piece of helpful information she shares.

Gerber brings discipline and wisdom to her words about responding to infant crying. Although she certainly agrees with mainstream advice on responding as quickly and consistently to infant tears as possible, she also offers solace to parents by admitting that responding quickly all of the time is practically impossible. Gerber's lack of urgency is markedly different from the tone found in many books for parents. One of the gifts Gerber brings to families is her attempt to relieve some of the pressure. She acknowledges a variety of positive approaches for meeting babies' needs and emphasizes that life won't come to an end if the baby periodically suffers a few unmet needs. She suggests that babies may learn important lessons by waiting every now and then or experiencing frustration.

In her writing and teaching, Gerber was very confident about the RIE methods and their success here and abroad. She did not expect everyone to agree with her, however. She described meetings with parents who expressed interest in RIE, but for whom the method was not a good match. Gerber wasted no time in telling the family just that. Observers have said that Gerber delivered her message with empathy and firmness, knowing many ways can help babies become attached.

Gerber coined the term *educarer*. She believed we need to care while we educate and educate while we care. It is not a term that the profession readily adopted, but its premise is a strong one, and one used by many child care teachers. Gerber stressed restraint as a way of respecting babies. She strongly objected to providers and parents treating new babies as objects. I thought of Gerber's work last year when I visited an accredited center and observed teachers walking around a crowded room of babies, popping bibs over their heads in preparation for lunch. They spoke to each other about details of their routine while simply doing what they needed to do for the babies, as if they were working with plants or photos or inanimate objects. I was distressed—like Gerber, I feel that this approach is more common than any of us want to believe. Gerber's goal was for adults always to tell a baby what was about to happen before it happened.

Several principles animated Gerber's RIE approach:

Active Participant: Babies need to become part of their routines, not to passively receive them.

Sensitive Observation: Understanding what the baby needs can be achieved only by carefully watching and listening to her.

Consistency: Clearly defined limits and expectations from the beginning help to develop positive discipline.

Basic Trust: The child needs to be an initiator, explorer, and self-learner.

Environment: Babies need spaces that are physically safe, cognitively challenging, and emotionally nurturing.

Uninterrupted Play: Babies need time alone to play on their own, at their own pace.

Freedom: Babies need to explore and interact with other babies.

Perhaps Gerber's most important emphasis is about time. We seem to be always in a hurry in this country. Babies, in order to form strong attachments, need to gaze into the eyes of people who are crazy about them. They need adults who can live with them in the moment.

Infants believe they are safe and competent when they have adults who can feel that way themselves. In order to feel that way, Gerber suggests that adults need to "do less and observe more." This takes time.

We need to give ourselves and the babies we love the gift of time—our time and their time. In Gerber's own words, "If you pay half attention—which nobody does, it's usually much less—but let's say you give half attention all the time, that's never full attention. Babies are always half hungry. But if you pay full attention a little bit of the time, then you go a long way. That's what I would recommend: to be fully with a child, then let her be" (1988).

Suggestions for Further Reading

Gerber, Magda. 2003. *Dear parent: Caring for infants with respect.* Los Angeles: Resources for Infant Educarers.

Petrie, Stephanie, and Sue Owen. 2006. *Authentic relationships in group care for infants and toddlers: Resources for infant educarers (RIE) principles into practice.* London and Philadelphia: Jessica Kingsley Publishers.

Gerber, Magda, ed. 1997. *The RIE manual for parents and professionals.* Los Angeles: Resources for Infant Educarers.

Chapter 4: John Kennell and Marshall Klaus

Most of the richness and beauty of life is derived from the close relationship that each individual has with a small number of other human beings—mother, father, brother, sister, husband, wife, son, daughter and a small cadre of close friends. With each person in this small group, the individual has a uniquely close attachment or bond. Much of the joy and sorrow of life revolves around attachments or affectional relationships—making them, breaking them, preparing for them and adjusting to their loss caused by death.

—John Kennell and Marshall Klaus (1976)

Doctors John Kennell and Marshall Klaus have shared an extraordinary collaboration for more than thirty-five years. Both were pediatricians at Case Western Reserve University of Medicine in Cleveland, Ohio, when they coauthored *Maternal-Infant Bonding* in 1976. The book created quite a stir in both the medical and parenting communities. Many contend that it was responsible for several of the changes in birth practices over the next twenty years. Kennell and Klaus illuminated the physical and psychological processes that mothers and babies experience in the first moments and hours of life.

Kennell and Klaus are best known for their research on and advocacy for bonding and attachment between newborns and their mothers. *Bonding* usually refers to the emotional tie from parent to infant. *Attachment* usually describes the tie from infant to parent. Kennell and Klaus were interested in both.

Their work was undertaken at a time in American culture when hospitals, babies, parents, and research were ready to take a turn in a different direction. The Harlow monkey experiments in the 1950s had given credence to Bowlby's and Ainsworth's theories that attachment is essential to development and is based on emotional, not only physical, needs. The time had come to investigate how parent-to-infant attachment grows. Kennell and Klaus wanted to document what enhances and nourishes this bonding and what disturbs or distorts it. They described their theory as a study of attachment in the opposite direction.

In this same postwar period, Konrad Lorenz was developing his theory of imprinting. Studying baby birds, he discovered that they follow the first moving object they see and develop a strong attachment to it. This happens almost immediately; if the mother is not nearby, the chick will attach to whatever it sees, including inanimate objects. Lorenz's work suggests there is a critical window of opportunity for this imprinting to take place.

Kennell and Klaus take this idea of critical opportunity and apply it to the human infant. They suggest the first few hours after birth offer a similar bonding opportunity to human parents and infants. They do not propose that the opportunity is forever lost if not made during those first few hours, but they do believe any bond formed later may not be as strong. They suggest the strength of this immediate bonding protects the parent-child pair from certain "disorders of parenting" (1976). Such potential disorders are modeled, in part, on Harlow's observation that monkeys who do not experience good parenting are unable to mate or parent effectively themselves. The suggestion was made that in order to parent well, one needed to have been parented well.

Evidence to support Kennell and Klaus's theories exists. The evangelical spirit that was soon attached to the "bonding experience" led many parents in the 1970s to feel as if they had missed their child's opportunity to bond with them if their infant had been born prematurely, had special medical needs as an infant, or had been adopted. Kennell and Klaus then theorized a second stage of attachment, which offered parents and babies other opportunities to develop mutually loving and responsive relationships. This second-stage bonding occurred over the first several months of an infant's life and gave parents continued chances to bond if the initial opportunity had been lost to medical or other emergency situations.

Kennell and Klaus's work was being shared in the years when women's entry into the workplace was taking an unprecedented climb. If parents could not spend all of those early months in the company of their new baby, could a grandmother, child care provider, or neighbor bond with the baby? If such bonds occurred, would the baby be less attached to her parents? Objections to Kennell and Klaus's research were heard from many corners of academia. Sociologists were quick to say that it was dangerous to set up self-fulfilling prophecies.

One of the critical questions is whether the feelings parents have about the choices they make can exacerbate their already-challenging circumstances. It is probably safe to say that the research of Kennell and Klaus and the popularization of their thinking by the press caused unnecessary pain to many young families. Before people discussed bonding or critical periods, parents worried about their child's health (if a baby was airlifted to the best medical care available) but not about a missed opportunity to establish permanent baby-parent relationships.

Few would debate the fact that secure attachments are essential for healthy future relationships. The pertinent questions are ones of defining the critical period, determining the number of relationships that can help an infant develop loving relationships for a lifetime, and the consequences to infants of parental ambivalence. Jerome Kagan's work cautions us to balance our approach to include supports to all babies and parents in all emergency and nonemergency birthing situations (1998). Kagan refers to the "allure of infant determinism" that captured the imagination of many developmental psychologists as they researched critical periods for infant development. He also suggests that Kennell and Klaus did not have sufficient scientific conclusions to send many worried parents into a spin when they had missed those critical periods with their children. He believed Kennell and Klaus's sample did not warrant such provocative conclusions.

I would agree with Kagan that those of us involved in work with children and families need to be cautious with information that can have a more detrimental effect on families than we intend. This is the perfect example of the "historical nodes of worry" (Kagan 1998) discussed in the introduction. It is certainly an example of an idea the media got carried away with before its effect on families was adequately considered.

Kennell and Klaus had conducted cross-cultural research and were struck by the supports that new mothers in developing countries continued to enjoy, while in the United States childbirth had been turned into a mostly surgical procedure. Klaus and Kennell emphasize that many variables can contribute to a mother's failure to bond with her infant (1976). They propose that hospital practices in the United States that separated parents and infants contributed to the problem and that procedures designed to protect premature infants, including sending them to a special nursery where parents are not able to hold or touch them, does more harm than good. They concede that humans are capable of emotional as well as physical separation. They cite variables such as grief, depression, competing emotions, or marital problems as factors that may prevent optimal parent-infant bonding. At the time, the popular press did not pick up on these subtleties in Kennell and Klaus's theory.

I vividly remember a childbirth class reunion in 1977. One of the members in the group had given birth after an emergency C-section; following the surgery, her infant had been airlifted to another hospital. With little sensitivity, some of the other new mothers gushed on and on about their deliveries, being able to nurse immediately, and rooming in. Then one said abruptly to the young mother, "You missed the whole thing. It's almost like you didn't give birth!" The look on this mother's face as she held her tiny three-month-old "miracle" was heartbreaking. It is this kind of absolutist approach to thinking about birthing that puts parents of preemies, adopted infants, and others who carry particular emotional burdens at birth at risk.

They concede that humans are capable of emotional as well as physical separation. They cite variables such as grief, depression, competing emotions, or marital problems as factors that may prevent optimal parent-infant bonding.

Antonio Madrid and Dale Pennington (2000) assert, "Maternal-infant bonding, then, is a natural biological occurrence. If there is nothing separating mother and child during the period immediately following birth, either physically or emotionally, it will most likely occur. The likelihood of bonding taking place seems to have little to do with the personality of the mother. Neurotic mothers bond. Borderline Personalities bond. Criminals bond. It seems that failures to bond are almost always the result of accidents: either separation inherent in hospital practices or maternal-emotional distractions."

The effects of nonbonding are varied. Often these babies are more colicky, dislike cuddling, and are described as difficult to please by their mothers. Some studies suggest (Zero to Three 2007) that these babies have an above average inclination to "bond" with alcohol, drugs, work, or possessions in adult life. Often they report distant relationships with their mothers, but many also report that they eventually got past these difficult emotions and became friends with their mothers.

In the conclusion of *Maternal-Infant Bonding*, John Kennell and Marshall Klaus offer their hope for the future: "We foresee that in the future the professionals will turn over one of their traditional roles in caring for the infant and mother to other members of the family. . . . As health providers integrate new procedures for caring for the family in the hospital into the present complicated network of hospital care, it is essential that major advances and contributions of modern obstetrics and neonatology are not lost."

Kennell and Klaus urge that childbirth take place in the hospital but that the hospital offer a wide range of services to meet the special medical and personal needs of each parent and family. These should include surgical facilities for C-sections in cases of fetal distress. They suggest hospitals build family-friendly spaces in which babies can be born in the company of family and friends. The express concern is that women may turn away from inflexible hospital policies and seek out the ancient art of midwifery. For those with special needs, this choice could be tragic.

While I was preparing this part of the book, I visited the Family Center at Exeter Hospital in Exeter, New Hampshire. A registered nurse gave me a tour of the newly completed Family Center. Decorated in subtle earth tones, the beautifully appointed rooms offered family dining tables, pull-out sofa beds for family members, and menus that the mother and her family may order from as they await their new arrival. A kitchen where coffee is always on and cold drinks and ice cream bars fill the refrigerator is open to all families. Fruit bowls are filled, and packages of popcorn sit next to the microwave. Children are welcome, the nurse informed me, as long as they are supported by a friend or relative other than the mother's labor coach. The hospital offers each family prenatal classes, sibling classes, car seat safety classes, breast-feeding support classes, and infant massage classes. The hospital has a round-the-clock lactation "warmline" for mothers to call for breast-feeding support.

Back in the family rooms, where immaculate hardwood floors warm the environment and blend with the tasteful artwork, I was treated to and amazed by the piéce de résistance: behind the prints on the walls, which drop down at the flick of a switch, are all the necessary medical emergency equipment to support emergencies that might arise: emergency C-sections and neonatal interventions occur in the room. No longer is the mother rushed away from her family or the infant rushed away from the mother—the room is transformed into an OR.

In their 1976 book, Kennell and Klaus challenged hospitals to become more responsive to the needs of families. To see such state-of-the-art facilities in a small, seacoast town in New Hampshire gave me reason to believe that these two researchers, who devoted their professional lives to alerting the medical community to the importance of supporting families throughout the birth process, have lived to see their dreams realized.

Suggestions for Further Reading

Klaus, Marshall H., and John H. Kennell. 1976. *Maternal-infant bonding: The impact of early separation or loss on family development.* Saint Louis: Mosby.

Sears, William, and Martha Sears. 2001. *Attachment parenting: A common-sense guide to understanding and nurturing your baby.* Boston: Little, Brown.

Kagan, Jerome. 1998. *Three seductive ideas.* Cambridge, MA: Harvard University Press.

Chapter 5: T. Berry Brazelton

Normal babies are not all alike. However obvious, this fact is invariably overlooked by the literature for new parents.

—T. Berry Brazelton (1969)

Thomas Berry Brazelton was born in Waco, Texas, in 1918. His parents, Thomas Berry Brazelton and Pauline (Battle) Brazelton, hoped their son would grow up to become a physician. While a premed student at Princeton University, Brazelton enjoyed participation in several college theatrical productions and considered a career on Broadway. T. Berry Sr. and Pauline Brazelton were unenthusiastic about acting as a career and suggested to young Brazelton that if he wanted their financial support, he'd best concentrate on his premedical studies. Brazelton decided to heed their advice—and aren't we all glad!

Whether you know Brazelton from his cable TV program on Lifetime, *What Every Baby Knows* (1983–1995), or from reading about the Brazelton Neonatal Behavioral Assessment Scale (1984) in an infant development class, you know his name. An instructor for years at Harvard Medical School, Brazelton has published hundreds of scholarly articles. His important message about infants and parents is best known to the general public through his syndicated newspaper column, his contributions to *Family Circle* and other popular media, and his many books. A prolific writer, Brazelton is well known for his popular books *Infants and Mothers* (1983), *Toddlers and Parents* (1974), *Doctor and Child* (1976), *On Becoming a Family* (1981), *Working and Caring* (1985), *What Every Baby Knows* (1987), and *Touchpoints: Your Child's Emotional and Behavioral Development* (1992).

Perhaps you know Brazelton because you have gone through Touchpoints training and have learned to alert parents to their son's or daughter's growth and development before the next stage is upon them. Brazelton has been a passionate voice for children and families for more than fifty years. He is no stranger to Capitol Hill, where for decades presidents have called on him to speak to issues involving the next generation. He was a passionate advocate for the Family Leave Act, passed in 1993.

Educated at Princeton and Columbia University School of Medicine, in 1947 Brazelton began his pediatrics training at Boston Children's Hospital. He became aware of the tendency in the medical profession to focus on pathology, but he was far more interested in normal development. (This was long before the term *strength-based* made its way into textbooks.) Brazelton knew he wanted to focus on what was going well, not on what was going poorly. He wanted to study human beings, not medicine, so he decided to enter a residency in child psychiatry at Putnam's Children's Center in Roxbury, Massachusetts. Child psychiatry, like strength-based studies, was not yet popular in the medical field, but Brazelton was a man ahead of his time.

In 1951, Brazelton began research on parents and babies. He focused on babies' competencies, which had gone unnoticed by the medical community. He was the first to differentiate between babies' behavioral styles. He determined that there are three primary styles: average, quiet, and unusually active. This finding alone endeared him to mothers forever. Now a mother could go to a Sunday dinner with the family and have medical defense on her side. Her sister-in-law's quiet baby might be easier to handle right now, but her own "unusually active" baby was not hyper, naughty, or anything else—he was just "her baby," and he was fine.

Brazelton paved the way for infant providers to prepare parents for developmental changes. He has given us the tools and sometimes even the words to share how we can support a baby's growth and development with parents.

Brazelton was among the first to promote service to the whole family after a baby is born. His sensitivity to working parents, single parents, parents of preemies—all parents—as they tried to navigate the turbulent waters of social change in the 1970s and 1980s was extraordinary. I've mentioned before the evangelical nature of some of the parenting books of the last several decades; Brazelton has always been an exception. He has remained a voice of reason, keeping families close to the reality of parenting. In his 1981 *On Becoming a Family*, he writes: "Attachment to a new baby does not take place overnight. It is tempting for parents to believe that having a baby and bonding to it is instinctive and that everyone is 'ready' for the parental role when it comes. Young parents-to-be welcome the presently popular claim that if one does everything right at labor and delivery, immediate bonding to the baby will be assured and this bonding will be intensely rewarding. Delicious pictures of mother, father and a beautiful baby smiling further romanticized the parental role. To a very large extent, of course, bonding is instinctive, but it is not instant and automatic. In order to be aware of its complexities and possible pitfalls, one must see it as a continuing process."

In 1951, Brazelton began research on parents and babies. He focused on babies' competencies. . . . He was the first to differentiate between babies' behavioral styles.

Brazelton helps providers share the importance of parent-provider partnerships sensitively with parents. He gives us words to support young parents when they separate for the first time from their infant. He has been the foremost voice in openly discussing how difficult it is for parents to leave their infants in the care of others. He helps us, as teachers, find ways to communicate to parents that they are the most important people in their babies' lives. He shows us how to help babies attach to multiple caregivers while still loving their parents best.

This approach is one of the reasons Brazelton is loved by so many educators and parents. He is a quiet, charming man whose sensitivity to babies and their parents makes him America's own baby charmer. He is thoughtful, reflective, and observant on the subject of parenthood and its effects on babyhood. His Touchpoints program has trained infant providers around the country to better support infants and parents in the first caregiving arrangement.

In 1973, Brazelton and his colleagues published the Neonatal Behavioral Assessment Scale (NBAS), which uses information obtained from providing newborns with visual, auditory, and tactile stimuli to study their responses to the environment. The information alerts trained practitioners to very early potential developmental problems; most other assessments cannot be used until infants are several months of age. In typical Brazelton style, the NBAS can be used to support adoptive parents as well. It seems to be Brazelton's gift to anticipate the pieces that present challenges to infants and their parents and to provide appropriate interventions. The NBAS, which was revised in 1984, is now used all over the world.

Brazelton's contributions to America's children and families are so extensive that it is challenging to single out one or more here. Brazelton stands out particularly for recognizing that for decades, the medical and psychoanalytic communities have looked at the individual instead of the family group. Brazelton has tried to explain to families how child care providers are underpaid and overworked. He has tried to explain to child care providers how parents behave when they leave their babies in care, and that they sometimes use defense mechanisms that make them appear indifferent. In his understanding of parents and caregivers, he has brought providers and parents together to work as a team in nurturing babies.

Brazelton remembers a time when it was easier to be a parent. He knows the feeling of undivided attention from a parent, and he knows how difficult it is to provide that in the twenty-first century. He tries to work with things as they are without losing sight of how he wishes they could be. As he approaches ninety, he is still one of America's most passionate advocates for children and families. He fights for preventive care and urges politicians and citizens to know what we lose by not investing up front in the next generation.

Suggestions for Further Reading

Brazelton, T. Berry. 1992. *Touchpoints: Your child's emotional and behavioral development.* Reading, MA: Addison-Wesley Publishing Company.

Brazelton, T. Berry. 1985. *Working and caring.* Reading, MA: Addison-Wesley Publishing Company.

Brazelton, T. Berry. 1983. *Infants and mothers: Differences in development.* New York: Delacorte Press.

Part 2

Impact of
Attachment Theory

The fact is that go-to-work/stay-at-home decisions are economically and ideologically driven, institutionally based, and very personal. A wide variety of choices deserve full support (much more than they get) and produce fine kids.

—Janna Malamud Smith (2003)

The contributions of the theorists and scholars outlined in Part 1 have been enormous. These theorists have been pioneers in the study of infant behaviors. Yet many questions remain for all of us who work with and study the very young. These four seem primary to me when it comes to infant care outside the home:

- How has the research affected babies and their families?

- How has it changed our practice in caring for infants and their families?

- How can we best care for infants in child care?

- How can we support families with infants in child care?

To bring research into our work with infants and families, we need to think seriously about the bridge between theory and practice. Applying research to early childhood programs is additionally complicated by the fact that children and families are more diverse than any study group. As the expression goes, "One size fits nobody!" We need to remember that no information is a perfect fit or easily applied to every family's situation. We need to be conscious of the cultural implications of research. We need to be balanced and cautious.

It is essential when caring for very young infants that teachers view their job as working with families, not working with babies. Possibly no other time is as critical in developing positive parent-provider relationships. One of the most important tasks of an infant teacher is to nurture parent competence. This doesn't always come easily; it requires reflection. Our job as the babies' teachers is to work with families to nourish loving partnerships. For this reason, each of the chapters in this part discusses how programs can best support babies and how we can support families.

All of the theorists whose work was described in earlier chapters maintain that we get a true picture of the infant-parent relationship only when we observe it naturally, preferably in the family's home. It's important to remember this when you're tempted to assess the quality of a parent-baby relationship in the morning, when separation is challenging, or at the end of a long workday. Reliable conclusions about relationships cannot be reached on the basis of those tiny windows of time. Yet this is usually all we get. Few programs have the luxury of time or family service staff to conduct regular home visits. This is what makes ongoing communication such a necessity. To ease family transitions to group care, time for sincere and supportive communication is necessary.

The following chapters address the issues reported by both parents and infant teachers as the biggest challenges to their interactions with babies: how to deal with feeding, sleeping, holding, and crying. I will also explore separation and stranger anxiety and how to build confidence and competence in babies and their parents.

In this chapter, I will look at the impact of bonding and attachment research on the early childhood field and on the birthing process. I offer this brief historical view of hospital policies and procedures to heighten your awareness of the vast variety of birthing experiences and their effects on young families. When we provide infant care, we are welcoming families into our programs at a time of great vulnerability in their lives. It is a well-established fact that families in the United States have few support structures to help them make this huge transition in their lives. Infant teachers must be aware of the challenges these young families face. Understanding the issues as well as their effects on babies and families helps equip us with a flexible repertoire of strategies to assist babies and families in navigating this new territory.

Changes in How We See Babies

Prior to the work on attachment theory, much more emphasis was placed on the physical care of infants and less on the emotional development of newborns. When Bowlby and Ainsworth began their work with infants, they went against the existing beliefs of the medical and psychiatric communities. Many of us still have a grandma or auntie who cautions us, "That baby will be spoiled rotten and running the house if you pick her up every time she cries." In the not-too-distant past, it was frequently said that if a baby was dry, fed, and safe, the best thing to do was to leave her alone (Spock 1970). It was thought that paying attention to a baby whose basic physical needs had been met would later cause trouble in the form of demanding behavior. We now know that the opposite is true. Infants whose signals for attention are quickly and sensitively responded to end up confident that they have the ability to get their needs met. Thus they cry less than those who are not quite sure they can get a response from the significant adults in their lives.

More and more of the general public has begun to understand that close, loving relationships in early infancy have a direct influence on loving relationships for the rest of one's life. Over twenty years ago, Alice Honig wrote, "Secure attachments early in life are the keystone for ensuring children's mental health" (quoted in Honig 2002). Her perspective clearly echoes those of pioneering theorists Bowlby and Ainsworth, and it is as true today as it was in 1984.

As we learn more about babies and what they need, it becomes easier for parents and providers to do the things that nurture optimal development. It is a common sight these days to see parents with a baby cuddled close in an infant carrier, allowing for maximum proximity to and view of the parent, talking to their infants in soothing tones as they walk through the supermarket. It wasn't too many years ago that parents waited until their babies started cooing or imitating sounds before they engaged in the mutual dance of early language. Now both parents and providers tend to talk to infants from day one. Similarly, in the early 1970s it was common for infants to be confined to cribs and infant seats in group child care centers. It was usual for parents and providers alike to think that new babies had few skills at being human. The recent explosion of brain development and early infancy research has taught us that human infants are very competent in many ways from the day they are born.

Changes in the Birth Process

Bonding and attachment theory have had a huge impact on the birth process itself. The work of John Kennell and Marshall Klaus has contributed to this basic family support in a way that will affect families for generations to come. Their theories and research on parent-infant bonding brought about changes in American hospital processes that were long overdue.

In the early 1960s, many obstetricians still treated pregnant women as if they had an illness. Labor and delivery were controlled in a sterile environment. Pain management was primarily handled with drugs and was little discussed with the parents-to-be. Fathers or partners rushed the pregnant woman to the hospital, then were encouraged to return to work or buy cigars to share with friends when the whole thing was over. The nurse called them when the baby was delivered. General anesthesia or spinal block was the norm. Often mothers were in a drug-induced sleep throughout the birth and met their newborns hours later. Newborns were hurried off to the nursery, where nurses often gave them bottles of formula before their mothers ever held them. Babies were brought to the mother's room every four hours for a scheduled feeding.

Siblings were not allowed to visit, and fathers viewed their newborns through the glass window of the nursery. It was common for male newborns to be circumcised in the hospital unless they were Jewish or the parents had vocalized their objections to the procedure. Bathing, diapering, and feeding were primarily handled by the nursing staff, and young mothers were encouraged to rest. There was usually a day when the new mother could meet with the nurse to try to change the baby on her own. She was wheeled to the car in a wheelchair, and the nurse handed the newborn to the father (often the first time he'd held the baby), while the nurse helped the mother into the car, where the father would then hand over the baby for the ride home.

It is a wonderful thing for both infants and parents that today, when grandmothers share these stories with daughters or daughters-in-law awaiting the birth of a baby, the response is disbelief. So much has changed for the positive.

The work of Kennell and Klaus and others has revolutionized the approach to family-centered labor and delivery practices. Once the United States made the transition from home births to the more "modern" and "medically sound" hospital deliveries, it was no longer part of our culture to consider options for birthing experiences. While it is true that many infants would have died from complications at birth decades before were saved through readily available and competent care in the hospital setting, solving this problem created other ones, and so it was with the transition to hospital births and medicated delivery. The habit of whisking babies away to an infant nursery to be weighed, measured, circumcised (if the babies were boys), fed, rocked, and put to sleep by hospital staff rather than allowing them to spend time with family deprived infants and parents of important bonding experiences. Kennell and Klaus documented the positive outcomes for babies and their parents when the birth process is savored and not rushed (1976). After the researchers' bonding and attachment work was picked up by the popular press, changes began to appear in hospital policies that were much more supportive of all involved.

Today many women about to give birth have been planning, preparing, and weighing choices and methods of delivery for months. Families without specific medical problems or risk factors often choose home births. There are physicians and midwives who are eager to support families who make this choice. Families who choose hospital births know they can be in birthing rooms where spouse, partner, friends, and children are also welcome.

Many books are available to assist parents in making choices about their infant's birth process. Mothers anticipate the birth and feel more empowered than previous generations of women were able to. A comfortable and informed mother-to-be will do a better job with the birthing process than someone who simply surrenders the process to a physician. Many expectant parents come to the birth experience after attending classes to prepare them for the event on many levels. Hospitals sponsor programs for siblings to ease this major change in a family system. Parents are informed about medication and have choices about the extent they wish to have medication as part of pain management. Birthing classes are open to all who wish to prepare for an unmedicated delivery.

The birthing process has returned, appropriately, to being viewed as natural and accomplished with lessons learned in birthing classes and support from loved ones. It is accepted practice for the mother to have a labor and delivery coach who shares the weeks of preparation and birthing classes. It is also an accepted and welcome fact that this coach can be the baby's father, a friend, the woman's own mother or grandmother—whomever the new mother feels comfortable sharing the experience with. The coach is welcomed and supported by hospital staff throughout the process.

Most hospitals today have birthing rooms in which the expectant mother settles for labor, delivery, and her first days with her child. Rooming in was established to allow a new mother to keep her infant at her side from the moment of birth. This arrangement allows her to feed on demand, to respond immediately to her infant's cues, and to spend uninterrupted time staring into her baby's eyes and enjoying the wonder of it all. A mother can now cuddle, touch, massage, and get to know her baby in ways that help mother and baby in the weeks and months to come.

The birthing process has returned, appropriately, to being viewed as natural and accomplished with lessons learned in birthing classes and support from loved ones.

The practice of allowing mothers choices in care and access to their newborns is now well entrenched in our culture. In fact, as insurance companies have urged shorter and shorter stays after birth, consumer and child advocates have pushed back, demanding the best possible start for infants and families. Birthing centers listen to families while they partner with them in the births of their children.

Supporting Families

It is a hallmark of the early childhood field to use the words *family support, parent involvement,* and *partnership* when we discuss our work with children and families. Unfortunately, the extent to which these principles are carried out in practice varies greatly. It is fair to say that this piece of our professional training was ignored for many decades. The past few decades have given us much more information on the importance of real partnering with parents—but it is also true that most of us have a long way to go in terms of supporting children in the context of their families. Years ago, Bettye Caldwell and Asa G. Hilliard compared child care to the extended family: "Professional child care is not a substitute or a competitor for parental care. To some extent, professional child care represents a version of the extended family which has adapted to the social realities of the modern world" (1985, 4). More recently, Anne Stonehouse has gone so far as to say, "Relationships between parents and teachers, perhaps more so than the activities and experiences offered to children, are likely to be a major determinant of the long-term impact on children of participation in early childhood programs" (1994, 2). We bear a major responsibility as early educators to take our work with parents just as seriously as we do our work with their little ones.

There are many ways we can do this right from the beginning. Here are a few of them:

- Inform yourself about the wide range of choices currently offered to families for their children's care. Read parenting books and magazines as well as those from the early childhood field.

- Support families' choices, especially if you disagree with them. Recognize your own biases, and try to transcend them.

- Increase your tolerance for ambivalence.

- Make parent communication an ongoing part of your professional planning time. Try very hard to respond to parents' needs when they come up spontaneously.

- Learn about and try to understand the variety of defense mechanisms at play when parents must share their brand-new baby with you.

Inform Yourself

One of the most significant areas in which infant caregivers can help families is in being more informed and responsive to the current high level of information and choice available to families in our culture. When we present any of the options—rooming in, baby massage, nursing, family sleeping, or other care for babies—as essential to an infant's well-being, we make it difficult for families who adopt, have preemies, have newborns with serious medical conditions, or have any number of cultural or family reasons why a perceived choice does not work for them. In the shadow of our certainty about particular methods, new parents can struggle terribly to develop necessary, positive esteem.

For example, when the wave of media about bonding and attachment experiences hit the popular press in the 1970s, it was often presented as if those who missed their window of opportunity for early bonding and attachment were doomed to less comfortable and less secure relationships with their children than those able to spend the first hours and days in constant connection with their infants. If you understand all the options available to parents and are familiar with the usual reasons (personal, cultural, medical, or otherwise) why any of them may be appropriate to a particular family, you're less likely to be surprised or taken aback when someone makes an uncommon choice. If you read the materials new parents are encouraged to turn to for advice, you're more likely to understand the barrage of information they are subjected to and sympathize with their courage in finding their way through it. This is equally important for caregivers who have given birth themselves and those who haven't. Teachers who haven't given birth may be surprised at the confounding array of choices and the complex factors that influence any family's decisions; teachers who have made their own choices in the birth process may find new information to help them understand why other choices might be better for someone else.

Support Family Choice

As early educators, our sphere of influence is great. We may work in a preschool program, but because of our degree in child development, we may find ourselves in a position to support families as they make birth choices. Early Head Start programs have direct influence because they work with prenatal mothers in the months leading to birth. Teachers discussing birth experiences in staff lounges can have a more significant influence on each other than they often realize.

We need to be able to discuss the ideal within a realistic context that offers support and encouragement to those families for whom the ideal is unrealistic. We also need to understand that there is no one ideal when it comes to birthing or parenting. There is an overwhelming sense of agreement among most mothers in the United States that they are constantly barraged by criticism of their ability to mother well and that encouragement comes less frequently and in smaller amounts. Early educators can carefully choose words to build parental self-esteem. We can model and verbalize the well-founded principle that development differs and that many ways exist to support those differences. We can help parents avoid comparing their infants, allay fears about delayed development, and assure parent groups that there are many paths to raising a child well. All parents travel their paths in their own way and on their own timetable.

People are different. What makes each of us comfortable or uncomfortable is unique to us and our situation. Some of us have high thresholds for pain while others of us don't. Similarly, choosing a medicated or unmedicated delivery is a very personal decision. Accept that home births, prepared childbirth, C-sections, hospital births, and midwife- and physician-assisted births are all options that result in fine births and fine babies. Accepting their choices helps parents feel empowered in making good decisions for their families. We want to bring a listening ear to the parents in our programs. Supporting their choices, not suggesting our choices, is the way to be helpful.

Be aware of your own biases, and remind yourself that expectant parents are vulnerable to family traditions, traumas, labor and delivery tales, and medical advice from great-aunts that can affect the direction they move in when planning a birth. For example, young, healthy women are usually excellent candidates for home births, but if an aunt died during delivery (possibly due to medical issues unrelated to the location of the birth), it is understandable that having grown up listening to the sad story told and retold, a young woman might choose an elective C-section or at the very least a hospital delivery.

When I gave birth for the first time in 1970, I was far away from my family, fathers were not allowed in the delivery room, and I was scared. When the staff nurse came in to check on me, I confided that I was really in pain. She didn't even look at me when she said, "Yeah, well, that's why they call it labor. It's work. It's supposed to hurt!" The isolation, loneliness, and fear I was experiencing magnified what was already difficult. A little encouragement would have gone a long way.

Encouragement and support are what we can contribute to the young families in our programs. It's not up to us to share fears that home births are unsafe, hospital births too rigid, or whatever personal opinions our own life has led us to. On the contrary, stopping in our busy day to listen can help. Touching a hand or saying something like, "Yes, there are so many choices today. It can be a real challenge to narrow the field. You still have several months, and I'm sure you'll settle on what feels best for your family," can ease the stress for an expectant family. Easing stress for expectant families should be one of our professional goals whenever we ponder the structures that start babies on the right path even before they are born.

We can model and verbalize the well-founded principle that development differs and that many ways exist to support those differences.

Tolerate Ambivalence

Gwen Morgan, professor emeritus at Wheelock College in Boston, once reminded me that we work in a field that is both complicated and complex. She said the complicated can always be simplified, but the complex must simply be coped with. She believes that too many of us for too long have been trying to simplify the complex rather than developing coping strategies and accepting what cannot be changed.

In her view, *complicated* refers to processes or decisions that may have many steps or stages but can have a simple outcome or one right answer. *Complex,* on the other hand, refers to processes or decisions that are morally, ethically, or philosophically ambiguous. There is no right answer; there may not be any solution that meets all the needs; there may only be the best you can do in the moment. Trying to create a simple, one-size-fits-all solution to a complex problem often means imposing arbitrary, rigid limits that make sense only some of the time. Many situations involving children and families fall into this second category.

A decision about using child care is both complicated (in terms of logistics) and complex (in the sense that there probably is no perfect option). For example, Roman and Martina live in Boston. They are expecting their first child, and both have high-paying professional jobs. They have a complicated array of child care choices before them. They have to consider logistics like cost, proximity to workplace (hers or his?), and the hours they need child care. At the same time, their decision is also complex. Should they choose a small family child care program, or a well-known large center like KinderCare? What about Martina's aunt Carrie, who has offered to take care of the baby for practically nothing? Would it be better for the baby to be with family who share their cultural background, in a family child care home with older children, or in a center with an amazing environment for infants and toddlers? If the baby goes to Aunt Carrie, will the transition into preschool be harder? There is so much to think about—and each possibility involves trade-offs. There is no one right answer and no solution without some costs. Each of their choices will produce differing outcomes for Roman and Martina and the baby. Their situation is complicated by having many choices, and it is also complex, because it can't be boiled down into a simple, right-or-wrong decision.

Now let's look at a completely different scenario. A nineteen-year-old single father with few financial resources, Jake has far fewer choices. His daughter's mother decided six months into the experience that parenting was not for her. She took off. No one knows where she is. Jake lives in a rural area and was recently laid off from his job. His car has been repossessed. He can walk to Early Head Start. He is income eligible. The only other infant care program is two towns away, and he has no transportation. However, he could also choose to leave Jessie with his neighbor, Brenda, who has an unregistered family child care home. He has only two options, and both are relatively simple—his situation is not complicated. However, his is still a complex decision. Is it more important that Jessie be in a formal, licensed program with trained and educated staff members, or would it be better for her to be in a home more like her own? If Jake feels comfortable with Brenda, whom he's known since he was a preschooler himself, should that figure into his decision? What if he gets a night job? Jessie can stay with Brenda whenever he works, while Early Head Start has more limited hours. Early Head Start offers him more resources for parenting and connecting to other parents. Either choice will have a different outcome for Jake and Jessie; both outcomes might be equally good, but they will be different. It's easy to see that even though Jake's choice is less complicated than Roman and Martina's, it is just as complex.

Early childhood programs are very similar to these two examples in their mixture of complications and complexity. They have many complicated but not complex logistical problems that can be simplified. But much of our practice is genuinely complex and can't be simplified—there are different ways to solve problems, with different results for children, families, and programs, but no right ways. In the past, unilateral decisions were sometimes made on the basis of knowledge we considered current "best practice" in our field. Today as we carefully weigh our decisions for children in the contexts of their families, cultures, and communities, it is much harder to decide what is most appropriate.

A ready example is toileting practices. There was a period of time when all of the best practice information early educators received came down on the side of "later is better." We were trained to counsel parents to wait for signs of readiness. Today we know that children can learn to sit on the toilet at an earlier age. Some families use American Sign Language with babies who can't yet verbalize their need for the toilet. Refugee and immigrant families may bring a different set of expectations to this task of life and childhood. Our best choice is to be more flexible and aware than we were in decades past. As Anne Stonehouse says, "Looking at the child in context means acknowledging the cultural background, and accepting the culture-bound nature of what we know about child development and what we believe about best practice with children" (1994, 2).

In many cases, in an attempt to simplify what is genuinely complex, child care providers have acted as if there is only one way to do things best for all babies. We can better do our jobs by recognizing and affirming the complexity of the choices now open to parents. Then we can support parents as they make the choices that best fit them and help them feel good about those choices. We can also affirm for those parents facing tough neonatal issues that they can assert their need to decide what is best for their child and expect the medical and child care communities to respect and support those choices.

Communicate with Parents

When infants are in group care in the early months of life, infant teachers must know how to support the whole family during this important transitional time. One of the most important ways to do this is to talk with parents so they become partners before day one of the child's experience in group care. Early educators are in a position to transform infant care practices and family life by acquiring the best current knowledge about babies, sharing that information with parents, and then acknowledging and affirming parents' decisions.

It is important for practitioners to remember that we can help parents anticipate and recognize developmental milestones in their children. Sometimes we become so immersed in or excited about our own work that we assume everyone else is keeping abreast of all of the changes in our field. I frequently hear child care teachers say something like, "How could she not know the baby was teething? She is a lawyer, for crying out loud!" We don't expect a plumber to know how to fix the engine on our Honda. We don't expect our physician to fix our air conditioner. We all have different areas of expertise. Part of an early childhood educator's expertise is knowing what to expect from babies. It is part of our job description to sensitively share these details with parents and not to judge them as incompetent because they don't already know.

Infant teachers also have the responsibility to keep parents informed about the baby's schedule, food intake, bowel movements, and sleep patterns. Sharing the details of the baby's day is helpful. Careful consideration should be given to the way information is shared. Many programs find written notes in the practice of quick forms or checklists helpful. Photos of a smile, a peaceful sleep, or a hearty approach to squashed bananas can also help parents see that their child, who struggles with separation in their presence, really does have fine days with his child care provider.

Time for communication with parents is extremely important. The younger the child, the more important this communication is. Ask parents what kind of schedule works for them. In group care, communication is often difficult because the long day usually means different staff welcome the baby in the morning than greet parents at the end of the day. Some child care programs schedule teachers on a four-day week. This still means the baby and family have multiple teachers, but a rotating schedule allows the same person to be with the baby all day. This is one of those dilemmas Gwen Morgan might refer to as complex—given the length of the working day for parents and teachers, it is impossible to make sure that the same person always sees parents and children at both ends of the day every day. We need to find coping strategies within our programs and our relationships with parents, because the length of day in care is not something providers or parents have much choice over.

Again, what is important here is not how communication is accomplished but that it is accomplished at all. Teachers frequently feel frustrated that arrival periods are busy and they don't have adequate communication time with parents. Sometimes we forget to brainstorm alternative strategies. Perhaps an evening call can make your relationship with a family blossom. I've heard teachers respond to a similar suggestion with, "I don't work after hours!" This is certainly a legitimate point. However, if your frustration level would lower and your quality of services would improve by working communication issues out in this way, it might be worth the investment. Sometimes arrival schedules are simply accidental. If all parents would feel better by having improved communication time with you, talk to your parents as a group and figure out how each can cooperate in order to make improvements for all. Talk to other teachers. How do they manage it? Talk to your families. What works best for them? Sometimes we assume a lack of interest when the real problem is a lack of communication. Sometimes the barrier can be defense mechanisms that parents put up in order to survive the pain of separating from their babies. For the competent infant teacher, becoming a detective to find out what the barriers are is essential. Then you can work with families or other staff to insure good communication with all families.

Understand Defense Mechanisms

Anyone who has worked in the early childhood field has heard teachers make comments about their frustrations with parents. "The children are fine—it's the parents that make me want a different line of work!" What is it that makes this so common in our field? There are too many reasons to list here, but the one I'd like to focus on is parents' defense mechanisms. Dr. Brazelton claims their use is alive and well among employed parents of very young children. According to Brazelton, parents need these defense mechanisms to survive the necessary separations from their babies (1988).

Brazelton understands that the field of early care and education suffers from low salaries and extreme demands. He also knows that it is difficult for teachers who labor hard all day at very demanding work and then greet parents who seem to be too busy to hear about their child's day not to blame those parents or consider them indifferent. He challenges us to see that parents forced by economic or other circumstances to work away from home and leave a six-week-old baby in the care of others suffer and grieve. By the late 1980s, it took two parents working full-time to have the same standard of living their parents enjoyed a generation ago on one salary (Brazelton 1988). We act as if parents could choose to be home or to work in order to take Disney vacations, when the reality is that today's parents work to provide food, heat, and clothing for their children. Few would debate that the financial considerations today are even severer than in the 1980s. Parents don't usually talk to us about these things. It is easier to act as if all is well and it doesn't matter. Brazelton urges us not to be fooled by this bravado. Brazelton suggests that today's parents carry unconscious anger about these conditions of their lives. They feel guilty about the time they spend away from their children, and the only way they can cope with their feelings is with defense mechanisms. He identifies three defense mechanisms that are universally employed by parents of young children to survive their day-to-day work:

- **Denial:** Refusing to look at the reality of the conditions and the toll it takes on their family life.

- **Projection:** Putting their feelings on others. Brazelton claims projection can be positive or negative. In other words, parents may think the provider is better for their child than they are (positive feelings, projected), or they may question the competence of the caregiver (negative feelings, projected).

- **Detachment:** Refusing to get too close, not because they don't love their baby but because they love her so much they can't bear the separation. To cope with these feelings, they become detached (Brazelton 1988).

If you are an infant teacher wanting to give the babies and families in your care the best start, watch for these typical parental responses, expect them, and develop strategies for dealing with them. You can help the parents move in a positive direction using true family support.

Since the United States does not have policies in place to support young families with paid time off and assured return to the workplace after giving birth, families must make hard decisions without much help or support. A number of leaders in our field, including T. Berry Brazelton, have suggested that a family be given a minimum of three months off after a birth or adoption to allow the family to get to know each other. The most common maternity leave in this country is three to six weeks. For this reason, one of the most significant things infant teachers can do to assist families with the transition to child care for their newborn is to understand the pain involved in the separation and the defense mechanisms that are common and necessary ways of dealing with these intense and difficult feelings. If a baby's parents are in the throes of denial or projection, don't take this personally. Remember where this comes from and why. Work to be sincere and honest with parents so they won't feel as much need to detach from their little ones.

Time for communication with parents is extremely important. The younger the child, the more important this communication is.

Supporting Babies

In the very beginning of our relationships with babies and their families, supporting babies and supporting their families is essentially the same thing. Some of the best ways to support babies look familiar from the previous section:

- Recognize that babies can attach to several significant adults.

- Create meaningful partnerships with babies' parents.

- Carefully observe babies during the initial weeks to determine what approaches work well, then compare these notes with the babies' parents.

- Serve as a translator for parents so they begin to know what their infants' signals mean. Talk. Share. Talk some more.

- Give parents information about bonding and attachment. Help parents understand their importance.

If these seem like additional ways to support families rather than specific strategies for supporting babies, that's because in the first weeks of life, supporting babies is really all about supporting their families. Brazelton makes his own distinction between bonding and attachment. He says that bonding is like falling in love, and attachment is about staying in love. He uses words like commitment and hard work to describe getting to know and interpret babies' behaviors. He encourages us to become experts at sharing the lives of new babies with their parents. He reminds us that the best way we can support the growth and development of new babies is by nurturing parental self-esteem and supporting the family unit (1992).

Early educators are in a wonderful position to help young parents feel comfortable about their child's growth and development:

- We can point out that tearful separations in the morning are an indication of the love and relationship between infant and parent.

- We can prepare parents for coming advances in their baby's skill level.

- We can encourage parents to call frequently if they are concerned about their baby's day.

- We can take time to schedule a conference if we see that the parents' comfort level does not ease with time.

- We can share happy photos from the baby's day.

- We can share information in a brief and readable form that helps parents understand the changes in their baby.

- We can make comfortable areas in our programs where parents can congregate, observe, and feel part of the out-of-home experience in their infants' lives.

Notice that all of these techniques are really about building relationships with families. In the beginning of care, with very young babies, that's the most important thing. In the next chapters, we'll talk more specifically about attachment theory and infant development.

Discussion Questions

1. Early educators have long desired excellence in their programs for infants and young children. Talk with colleagues about the notion that we need to be able to discuss the ideal within a realistic context. What do you think this means? Give an example.

2. When you gave birth to your second child, it was a home birth. Your three-year-old bounced in and out while you labored to deliver her brother. It was a natural, memorable family experience. You speak often of the joys of home births. Nine-month-old Sara is in your group at the center. Her mom, a realtor, has won a week in Mexico the month after her due date with Sara's sister. She's pondering an elective C-section two weeks before her due date so she won't miss the trip. She asks what you think. What do you say?

3. Early educators are in the position to share information and resources with new parents. What is the significance of personal opinion to these discussions? Are there boundaries that shouldn't be crossed? Who determines them? What role do you think your personal opinion plays in your work with parents? Why? Give a concrete example.

Suggestions for Further Reading

Crittenden, Ann. 2001. *The price of motherhood: Why the most important job in the world is still the least valued.* New York: Henry Holt and Company.

Douglas, Susan J., and Meredith W. Michaels. 2005. *The mommy myth: The idealization of motherhood and how it has undermined women.* New York: Free Press.

Malamud Smith, Janna. 2003. *A potent spell: Mother love and the power of fear.* Boston: Houghton Mifflin.

Chapter 7: Infant Care Practices

The most important thing I have to say is that you should not take too literally what is said in this book. Every child is different, every parent is different, every illness or behavior problem is somewhat different from every other.

—Benjamin Spock (1970)

These words introduce Benjamin Spock's third edition of *Baby and Child Care,* published in 1970. It is the first of many humble statements on the part of the good doctor that apologize for having spoken with such certainty in 1945, when the book was first published. In this country, in the not-too-distant past, young parents looked only to their own parents and a pediatrician, or "Dr. Spock," to know what to do with their new baby. Hospitals did not require or even offer prenatal classes. We did not have huge malls or large bookstores with row upon row of books targeted at helping parents raise their children. I once commented to my daughter-in-law that it is now such an exciting time with so many resources for young parents that I envied her. Only Spock's *Baby and Child Care* was available when I was pregnant. T. Berry Brazelton had just published *Infants and Mothers,* but it took awhile for it to become established on the bookshelves next to Spock. (My daughter-in-law quickly responded that that might be true, but it can be overwhelming today to walk into a huge bookstore and be ushered to the parenting section, which seems to go on forever.)

My enthusiasm for Spock's and Brazelton's books is prompted by their clear messages to the families of America that there are differences in development. Prior to their books hitting the popular press, media stressed "a baby should" or "a baby shouldn't" without reference to which baby or under what circumstance. Every auntie, whether she had raised children or not, had strong ideas about bedtime, feeding, crying, and toilet teaching. Young parents often benefited from access to extended family, something that fewer young families experience today. But there was also tremendous pressure to do "what we did." The conventional wisdom of the times held that mothers and grandmothers knew what was best. People didn't know much about temperament at the time and frequently credited infants with thought processes that we now know don't exist in infancy—for example: "Every time you pick her up like that when she's whimpering, you are just giving her more power. She already knows she's got the upper hand." Many an insecure young mom heard this kind of comment from her mother or grandmother in the 1960s or 1970s.

Just as with birthing information, the explosion of research on brain development and marketing to new parents in recent decades has made much more information accessible. The new baby classes sponsored by hospitals and communities have also made a difference.

This chapter will address three of the four big concerns most new parents have: feeding practices, sleeping, and holding. The fourth, infant crying, is so complex a topic that a separate chapter has been devoted to it (chapter 8). These four areas create ambivalence, points of disagreement, and discussions with both generational and cultural overtones.

Feeding Practices

It is an exciting step forward for babies in the United States that, depending on whose statistics you are using, between 70 and 90 percent of young mothers are nursing. There is no doubt that breast milk is the best possible choice for newborns. Babies are not allergic to breast milk. Breast milk fortifies newborns against disease and upset stomach. Today physicians and attending pediatric nurses encourage mothers to nurse. Beyond the merits of perfect nutrition, the benefits of nursing to the mother-infant relationship are enormous. The skin-to-skin connection enhances the loving relationship. The fact that the nursing mother cannot delegate this task ensures that this special time will be a regular part of the day for her and her baby. The holding and gazing that go on throughout the process enhance the developing relationship, contributing positively to the attachment between the pair.

At birth, before the breast milk comes in, colostrum is available to the baby. Colostrum is full of minerals and important antibodies that give the baby a healthy foundation before actual feedings become established. Breast milk is easy to digest, is the right temperature, takes no preparation, is easy to transport, and is readily available.

T. Berry Brazelton (1992) reports that mothers returning to work shortly after giving birth are increasingly choosing bottle-feeding over nursing. When he talks with these mothers, they often express fears of becoming too attached to their babies. Brazelton suggests that all of us who work with infants and parents do as much as we can to encourage nursing and support the family. He believes that coming home after a hard day's work and settling into a rocking chair, nursing and singing to her infant, is the best thing for the mother and her baby.

Remember that it was less than a century ago that the early attachment theorists still linked positive relationships between babies and mothers solely to nursing. It wasn't until Harlow's studies with monkeys in the 1950s that the research community documented the comforting behaviors of adults toward their young as significant parts of caring. So it is understandable that the controversy still flares regarding choices to breast- or bottle-feed. For early educators the critical piece is family support. We need to support all babies and their parents as they choose among the myriad feeding challenges during the earliest weeks and months of life. We need to respect each family's choice for their baby.

There are many reasons why a family may choose not to breast-feed. Sometimes there is no choice at all: medical emergencies that require separation of moms and infants, infant adoption, medication needs of mothers that make breast-feeding impossible or unsafe, and jobs involving long commutes or working conditions that don't support a nursing schedule are the primary "non-choice" reasons. Low milk supply does not get much attention, but it is also a factor in whether women nurse or not. A range of social or cultural factors can also affect the decision. Often a young mother's own mother's strong feelings about one choice over the other becomes the determining factor. For some people, there are leftover stigmas associating nursing with poverty. In the 1940s and 1950s it was considered the affluent choice to bottle-feed. For several decades, bottle-feeding was the norm unless families were living in poverty and couldn't afford the more expensive, modern alternative to nursing. The critical point for educators to remember is that every family's choice needs our respect and support.

If a mother returning to work six weeks after giving birth is bottle-feeding and discovers her baby has allergies to a particular formula, trying to find the right choice for her baby can be a frightening experience for her to go through. It isn't helpful if an infant teacher offers empathy for this difficult and emotional time and then concludes with, "That's why I always breast-fed my babies!" Many parents struggle with this choice, and once it has been made, if difficulties arise, the parents may feel guilt or remorse. This is particularly challenging for the mother who chooses bottle-feeding and encounters unexpected problems, because reversing the decision is not as easy as weaning baby from breast to bottle.

Parent and medical community debates over infant feeding have gone on publicly and with passion for years. They are likely to continue. Grandma, whose baby didn't gain enough weight, attributes it to nursing. In turn, she urges her granddaughter to bottle-feed so she can know how much the infant is drinking. The American Medical Association urges new mothers to nurse for health reasons. Most employers in our country do nothing to support nursing mothers in the workplace. Even some of our child care programs (which should know better) act in ways that subtly or not so subtly discourage new mothers from trying to nurse when they must return to the workplace quickly. The La Leche League, which offers support to nursing mothers, has been known to withdraw its support and become rejecting

As providers of care, we want to welcome all families to nurture their children in the way most comfortable for them. Then we want to support them in their choices.

if a new mother decides breast-feeding just isn't for her. The media report stories of young mothers arrested for indecent exposure for nursing in public. In our country, where a high tolerance for neon-lit breasts is evident in urban areas, we still have a lot of ambivalence about mothers and babies sharing this important experience.

Today there are many resources to help families make decisions about breast- and bottle-feeding. Family centers frequently have lactation specialists and nursing coaches on staff to help new mothers. Evangelical approaches to feeding, sleeping, and holding have been replaced with the more balanced position that we must support the family in their choice. As providers of care, we want to welcome all families to nurture their children in the way most comfortable for them. Then we want to support them in their choices.

British early educator Penelope Leach understood this perhaps better than anyone. She is one of the best models for providers to follow when they are considering how to support young families with babies. Leach combined her passion for promoting what is good for children with a sensitivity to their mothers: "Only you can decide whether to breast or bottle feed. It is your body and your baby. Nobody has the right to pressure you either way or to condemn you whatever you decide" (1978). This was Leach's courageous statement to young mothers in 1978, when diversity was not the driving force it is today. Many mothers then were as heavily criticized for bottle-feeding their infants as their mothers had been a generation before for continuing to nurse rather than join the modern movement to bottle-feed.

Penelope Leach was as certain that breast-feeding was the ideal choice for babies as the rest of the medical-psychological community. She had the presence of mind, nevertheless, to remember that there are differences in families, cultures, and individuals. She encouraged new mothers not to listen to the arguments of the pro-bottle/pro-breast camps but rather to ask themselves important questions like these:

- What kind of person am I?

- Am I easily embarrassed by nursing in public?

- Will I be able to transcend that feeling if my baby is hungry and I can't find a private space?

- Does my life lend itself easily to nursing?

- Should my child need special medical care, can I adapt to bottle-feeding?

- Does my partner feel left out? Should other adults offer supplemental feedings?

These questions help parents make the right decisions for their families instead of being influenced by even well-meaning people who don't have all the information that the families themselves do.

Attachment Theory and Infant Feeding

Attachment theorists agree that emotional development is enhanced during feeding. Magda Gerber reminds us to carefully observe the baby to determine her preferences for holding and eye contact during feeding times (2003). Brazelton counsels that encouraging nursing and offering supportive environments for parents to comfortably settle in for feedings is essential at our child care centers (1992). One of the interesting aspects of Kennell and Klaus's cross-cultural studies is the fact that in cultures where babies are fed on demand and have continual contact with their mother in an infant carrier, infants tend to have few of the gastrointestinal difficulties so common in the United States during the early months of life (1976). Many lessons from attachment theory can help us support infants and their families' feeding practices:

- Newborns need to be held and cuddled when feeding.

- Breast milk offers special health benefits to the newborn.

- Formula can be a very healthy and acceptable alternative to nursing.

- Infants benefit when their parents choose the feeding method most comfortable for them and their family.

- Since eye contact and cuddling are as essential as physical nourishment, the infant should always be held for feedings.

- Babies in infant care benefit from primary caregiving.

- Parents uncertain about their choices should begin by nursing, because mother and infant can easily switch to bottle-feeding, but it is not easy to switch back to breast-feeding from bottle-feeding.

Supporting Babies

Child care centers play an important role in establishing healthy routines for infant feeding. This includes creating comfortable spaces for nursing mothers, establishing healthy, nurturing feeding practices, and communicating with parents about their infants' progress. Putting these practices in place to support infants' feeding needs is an important part of our work with babies. Here are some ideas to consider regarding feeding times at centers:

- Calm environments promote healthy mealtimes.

- Assigning staff as primary caregivers supports all infant routines.

- Focused feeding times are essential.

Calm Environments

The rocking chair for infant feedings should be out of the way of hustle and bustle. Quiet music or just plain quiet can support positive infant feeding times. This is a time for eye contact, smiles, loving touches, and connection. Teachers who team in an infant environment need to discuss supporting each other by diminishing interruptions during this special time. Even details like soft colors in the infant room can contribute to the overall peace that accompanies important routines. Again, Magda Gerber's suggestions for thoughtful observation of babies' behaviors can tell us how much stimulation is too much, who likes conversation during feedings, and who prefers quiet.

Primary Caregiving

I visited a program recently in which babies were all fed by the same staff person. Diapers were someone else's job, and there were staff who acted as "rockers" and "walkers." It was someone's idea of efficiency, and it somewhat resembled a factory. I believe the most important lesson we have learned from attachment theory is that early relationships are one of the primary foundations of positive emotional development. Continuity of care is essential. What I hope to see when visiting an infant center is care centered on primary caregiving. With this practice babies can count on being fed, rocked, changed, sung to, and returned to family at the end of the day by the same special adult. Many centers have initiated forty-hour workweeks with ten-hour days on a rotating basis so babies and parents can experience just one adult in their daily routine.

Attachment theorists agree that emotional development is enhanced during feeding.

It's important that babies not be exposed to a continually changing cast of characters at the center. Contemporary attachment theorists assure us that infants can develop several strong attachments (for example, to grandma, dad, auntie, infant teacher, mom). Infant teachers can use this information to help reassure new parents. Babies in infant care should look forward to the comfort of the same smiling face as they move from sleeping to waking, from diapering to feeding times.

Just as putting infant needs ahead of parent needs is sometimes inconvenient, it is sometimes inconvenient to put infant needs ahead of staff needs at the center. Staffing needs are not as easily met when we provide primary caregivers, yet it is in the best interest of the babies in our care to arrange staffing to meet babies' needs for that one special person.

Focused Feedings

It is important to ready yourself for feeding times with the babies in your care. Have you taken your break? Have you been to the bathroom? Are the lights low, the music low or off? Do you have everything you need? Is the formula or pumped breast milk the right temperature? Do you have that blanket this baby likes to touch while feeding? Do your colleagues know you are about to enter into focused time? The answering machine can pick up calls if you are alone. This is time for you and baby, and (emergencies excepted) it should not be interrupted. Enjoying this routine is important for both of you.

Supporting Families

How can child care centers build on the work of T. Berry Brazelton and Penelope Leach to support family choices for feeding routines? Here are three important first steps:

- Arrange the environment.

- Welcome nursing mothers.

- Keep careful records.

Arrange the Environment

Just as Brazelton talks about the importance of parents focusing on babies when they connect at the end of the day, regardless of other tasks that await, so he reminds teachers that having a "parent friendly" environment is essential for infant teachers. It is a wonderful thing when infant centers offer spaces for nursing mothers. When space does not allow, having an emotionally soothing environment and attitude that welcome parents is the next best thing. Elements may include a rocking chair, a baby changed and ready to be fed by a parent on a tight schedule, and an accepting attitude when parents' schedules change and they arrive unexpectedly to feed their little one.

Welcome Nursing Mothers

Your parent handbook should include a section about feeding times that takes the guesswork out of the day for families. You can describe how feeding times happen during the day. You can ask parents about their and their child's preferences for feeding times. You can assure parents that breast-feeding is welcomed and you are eager to support them at the center. Providers of infant care can help families by providing comfortable spaces where mothers can nurse. Part of this includes having private places for mothers who need that privacy as well as being comfortable with the process and encouraging other families to accept this natural process as part of living with young children. Some mothers are comfortable nursing their infant while sitting on the floor in the toddler room, enjoying time with the baby's older sibling. Others will be happier if they can sit quietly in an empty classroom or even in the director's office.

Keep Careful Records

A final piece of supporting babies and parents around feeding practices at the center is keeping good records. It's important that parents and infant teachers work together to support infant development, and good communication (both verbal and written) should be a part of every day. How the baby slept or what kind of weekend he had may affect activity and hunger levels. If a pediatrician is worried about allergies, she may need your record of which foods are introduced when and how the baby reacted. If the baby ate

extremely well at noon and parents know it because it is in your
record of the baby's day, then they are less likely to be concerned
if she has little appetite at suppertime or late in the evening. Some
programs send notebooks back and forth every day so parent and
teacher notes are in the same place. The important thing, of course,
is not how it is done but that it is done.

Sleeping Practices

I still vividly remember the advice I was given when leaving the
hospital with my first child in 1970. "Put that little boy right in his
own room and let him understand that the separation begins now.
You'll never regret it!" All we can do is the best we can do with the
information we have at the time. That nurse meant well and thought
she was giving me sound advice. But she was wrong. Like many
young women at the time, I put too much emphasis on what medical professionals told me to do and did not trust my gut response
enough. I can remember the upset stomach I experienced, sitting on
the floor outside his little nursery, listening to him cry and wanting
to pick him up. But Dr. Spock said not to. My mother said not to.
My grandmother said he'd be ruling the house in a year if I let him
direct my behavior when he was only six weeks old. I wanted to
be a good mother. So I followed the program. He survived. So did I,
but I still regret it!

As with feeding, there isn't one answer in the question of what
to do with babies and sleep. There are many answers—and again,
those depend on the situation, the baby, and the family.

According to Zero to Three (2008), one of the most frequent reasons for night waking in young children is parents' overestimating
their child's need for sleep. This tends to be more of an issue in the
United States than in European countries. Other countries seem to
be more attuned to the individual differences in developing infants.

In this country, parents typically desire independence on the
part of even the youngest infants and expect them to sleep alone in
a room away from parents and siblings. This is a uniquely American
notion. Throughout history and currently around the world, children
have slept with others (sibling, parents, grandparents)—yet in this
country there is still much impassioned debate over the practice
of cosleeping. Remo Largo (1993) reports that children working on

attachments to their parents during the first year of life are lonely at night and don't know what to do when left alone. "Even today, millions of children in numerous cultures do not sleep alone. Yet in Western industrial societies, a misfit between culture and basic human needs has become the norm. For at least some infants and young children, being forced to sleep by themselves constitutes an unduly heavy burden" (1993). Largo makes the point that these same parents would never expect their children to spend several hours alone during the daytime hours.

When families of infants approach mental health workers for support about their child's sleep patterns during these critical early weeks and months of life, the outcomes are often very successful. Frequently clinicians suggest that parents keep a carefully monitored sleep log on their child's sleep patterns. When parents are able to see that their infant has stable patterns of sleep but fewer hours than the parent had expected, they can more easily adapt to their baby's individual patterns and needs.

This is an important strategy for infant care providers as well. I have often heard infant teachers bemoan the fact that one or two of the babies in their care just never sleep! When encouraged to keep a careful log, these teachers soon realize that their expectations are inappropriate for these particular children. It is important to emphasize that often when adult expectations are out of sync with a baby's natural rhythms, the adults experience frustration and impatience, and this tension is passed on to the infant when she is held by a tired, tense caregiver or parent.

When parents and providers have a strict idea of how the infant ought to respond at particular stages of development, they get into trouble. With sleeping, as with feeding and other essential components of living with babies, many models work. It depends on the child, the child's temperament, the parent or provider, and her match of style or model to that of the child. Rigid expectations can only frustrate the adult and complicate the child's development.

Attachment Theory and Sleep
Of the theorists I discussed in part 1, Kennell and Klaus and Magda Gerber provide the most help on the topic of sleeping practices. It is interesting that the practical implications of their work seem almost

at odds with each other in terms of translating attachment theory into practice. For infant teachers wanting to engage in supportive sleeping practices for babies, it's a good idea to ponder all of the theory and then adapt policies and practices to the particular children and conditions of your workplace and families.

Kennell and Klaus (1976) call public attention to the cultural differences in the approach to sleep between families in the United States and those around the world. They want to raise our consciousness to the fact that babies need comfort in the middle of the night and that parents provide comfort merely by being present. In many countries around the world, families sleep in a small amount of space. It is an American cultural construct that infants need their own space from the time they are born. This notion is slowly changing, as more and more young families become comfortable with sharing their rooms with newborns. For child care centers serving refugee and immigrant families, meeting requests for siblings to sleep together at naptime is becoming commonplace.

Magda Gerber focuses our attention on another dimension of this aspect of infant care. She believes we have gone too far in our attempts to keep infants within arm's distance at every moment. She asserts that it is truly the baby's job to learn how to fall asleep. She does not believe in putting the baby to sleep with a bottle or nursing. She does not believe rocking the baby to sleep is best. She believes putting the baby to bed while he is still awake is best because this allows the baby to know the routine of bedtime. She has been somewhat controversial in asserting that some babies really do seem to need to cry themselves to sleep, even though it is painful for parents to allow it. She is a proponent of an easygoing but predictable schedule for babies that allows them to calmly accept that going to sleep is one of their expected daily routines (1998).

For infant teachers, then, decisions about sleep policies are complex and must be made carefully, in cooperation with parents and after sensitive observation of the individual baby. When we assess the sleeping needs of infants as we understand them today, there are many things we can think about:

- Sleep needs of infants and toddlers vary greatly. At the same time, many books for parents assert that children need a prescribed number of hours of sleep each night.

- Many children do not sleep through the night every night until well into the third year of life.

- Sleep deprivation has a significant and energy-depleting effect on children and adults. Parents and caregivers of nonsleepers suffer energy depletion and loss of esteem as competent caregivers.

- Cosleeping with parents is a common practice in many cultures. Parents in the United States whose children consistently share their bed are often hesitant to admit it.

- When forming early attachments with significant adults, babies understandably resist separation at night.

- Keeping a sleep log can help parents and providers better understand a baby's actual sleep needs.

Supporting Babies

T. Berry Brazelton has given us excellent advice when it comes to our standard practices with infants: Observe! Observe! Observe! Each baby is different. Sleep practices often go hand in hand with temperament. Talk to families to find out as much as you can about the baby's habits at home. Watch the baby for signs of what makes her comfortable when approaching rest times. Magda Gerber reminds us that all the other routines of the day have an effect on how the baby settles at rest time. Gerber stresses the need for fresh air and activity, regular mealtimes and routines. She believes that grown-ups have to slow down to provide a calm environment for babies. When all these things are in place, Gerber believes, natural sleep routines will develop (2003).

It's a good idea to ponder all of the theory and then adapt policies and practices to the particular children and conditions of your workplace and families.

Practices for infant centers to support babies' sleep routines should include:

- A peaceful sleeping environment

- Careful attention to individualizing when possible

- Regular routines for settling

Provide a Peaceful Sleeping Environment

Many infant centers have separate sleep rooms for babies. These are darkened, quiet spaces that most of us consider conducive to peaceful sleep. If such space is not possible, separating waking spaces from sleeping spaces is critical. It is challenging to drift off to sleep with bright sunshine streaming through the window. Quiet lullabies often provide a soothing context for sleeping. Note, however, that there are cultural differences concerning where and when babies fall asleep. Some babies who are accustomed to being in the midst of an active, extended family group simply fall asleep whenever they need to, right in the middle of noise, light, and activity. Babies who are accustomed to sleeping with parents or siblings may have a difficult time napping alone in a crib. Room temperature should be cool but not cold or drafty. Soft sheets, comfy blankets, and a comfort item (if desirable) from home usually help. Magda Gerber reminds us that talking to the baby about time for rest should be part of sleep routines from day one (2002).

Individualize When Possible

Brazelton (1969) was the first to clarify for us that sleep needs vary a great deal, even among brand-new babies. We need to observe carefully, keep written records, and talk to parents about the baby's patterns when planning for sleep routines at the center. We should expect that the easygoing baby will probably establish "easy" sleep routines in a way that the fussier baby will not. The temperamentally challenging infant may well struggle with this part of her day, just as she does with feeding and other routines. She needs our loving support in a way that an easier infant does not. We need to be creative in our approach to these little ones. Swaddling (wrapping baby closely in soft blankets to reduce startling) is often a good approach. Soft music tends to have a calming effect on most of us. Make sure that activity levels are reduced slowly as naptime approaches. Finally, remember that no one can force anyone else to fall asleep. Set up a peaceful environment, establish regular routines, individualize when possible, and then, as Magda Gerber reminds us, it truly is up to the baby.

Use Regular Settling Routines

Somehow it never ceases to amaze me when I am observing in an infant room and another teacher walks in and says loudly to the infant teacher, "When is that in-service?" as if no one is trying to sleep! It is important for infant teachers to work with colleagues on respecting the quiet of an infant room. If you do not have a "Shhh! We are sleeping!" sign for your door, perhaps a sign is the first thing to make or acquire when establishing routines. Make it! Hang it! Talk to your colleagues about how difficult it is when people burst into the room while you are settling babies.

Establish a sleep-time routine with each child. Reading a favorite book (often the same one every day) to signal sleep times is helpful. Playing the same sleep music at rest times is soothing. Making your schedule as predictable as possible is helpful to older babies. Newborns are always on their own schedule anyway.

Plan your day so that exciting outdoor time or activities are not scheduled right before sleep routines. Talk to the babies all day about what is happening in order to help them integrate the routines. Slow your pace to help infants, even frantic ones, slow theirs. Learn the techniques that help each of your babies settle. Watch for signs of fatigue. Sing softly, rub heads and backs. Enjoy the quiet.

Supporting Parents

Only recently have the medical or early childhood communities given attention to the effects of sleep deprivation on families with young children. This is an area in which your energy with parents will have a direct effect on the babies in your care. Sleep deprivation is a terrible burden. When adults don't get enough sleep, they find it difficult to be effective parents. When they become exhausted and tense, their feelings can easily be passed on to their infants through a tense, exhausted embrace. To make matters worse, we don't do enough to inform parents about how varied babies' needs for sleep can be. So besides the stress of a screaming infant, parents have to deal with their worry that they must be doing something wrong. If we have had the good fortune ourselves of giving birth to easygoing infants, we need to offer empathy to parents of babies who don't sleep. If our experience was peaceful and we assume the parents of a stormy infant must be doing something wrong, then we become part of the problem when our job is to be part of the solution.

Here are some strategies to support parents:

- Provide information and resources.

- Listen attentively.

- Provide structures to ensure adequate verbal and written communication.

Provide Information and Resources

Despite all the progress made in recent decades to provide useful information to new parents, having a baby remains one of the most life-altering experiences a person can engage in. Even well-informed parents who have attended prenatal classes and read the latest books tend to find the initial weeks and months overwhelming. I have never met a new parent who is not surprised by the intensity of the positive and negative aspects of the experience. Infant teachers sometimes forget that no matter what books parents have read, their information base is still quite different from what anyone involved in child growth and development knows from experience. New parents are overwhelmed, sleep deprived, and very concerned about doing what is best for their baby. They need our support, understanding, and readable bites of information to make day-to-day life with their baby easier.

Part of helping can be as easy as providing updated resources in your community for La Leche League, pediatricians, emergency clinics, and parent groups. Look for brochures available from the National Association for the Education of Young Children (NAEYC) or other reputable sources that offer information on infant crying, sleeping, feeding, sudden infant death syndrome (SIDS), and family counseling. Put them in an easy to find spot (perhaps by the sign-in/sign-out sheets) where parents can pick up helpful information on specific topics without having to ask.

Listen Attentively

Most of us want to be heard. We often talk to make sense of what we are thinking. New parents, particularly mothers, are not so much looking for answers as they are for a place to share their questions. Though we have valuable information to impart with parents, it's also important for us just to listen, not make suggestions, and affirm to the parents that we have heard their concerns. As Brazelton points out, it is very common for new and stressed parents to project their feelings onto the baby's infant teacher. Sometimes "Are you sure she is comfortable here?" really means "Am I comfortable with my baby?" Sincerely expressing our confidence in the parent's ability is one of the best responses we can give to the parent's concern. Active listening (the process of repeating what has been said to clarify what we have heard and understood) is all that is needed. When a parent shares a concern, consider saying something like, "Wow, it sounds like you are really exhausted from being up so much at night. Those first months can be so hard." Wait to offer resources until you are sure the parents are looking for more than a friendly ear.

Provide Avenues for Communication

Closely related to attentively listening to parents is the skill of providing the right structures for communication between home and center. Sometimes this is easy—parents write volumes that we barely have time to read. Other times it can be hard. It is our job as early educators to assist parents in seeing the importance of two-way, ongoing communication. Teachers and parents need to keep each other informed as they work to understand what this little individual needs and what works best for *her*.

Some of the communication is technical. We want to keep parents informed of feeding times, sleep schedules, bowel movements, periods of extended crying, and other daily events in a baby's life. Anne Stonehouse (1994) suggests that we share a baby's movement toward developmental milestones but stop short of saying, "She rolled over today." This allows the parent to be the one to come to us with this big news. We want to have an ongoing exchange with parents that addresses changes in the baby's behaviors and our responses to those changes. It is extremely important to remember the value of sharing little stories about the baby's day so that when we ask parents to pause to chat, they are not anticipating problems. There is no greater gift to a working parent than a carefully prepared portfolio with wonderful photographs of the baby's days at the center!

Holding

Perhaps no issue has been quite so controversial as how much a baby should be held. It is frustrating for me to hear providers of infant care complain that this baby or that baby just wants to be held. Of course babies want to be held. Babies need to be held. There are many reasons for this. Holding is a primary way to offer love and security to an infant. An infant has no control over her own position, so if she is to get about and see things and find out what is going on, someone must carry her around. Proximity to the primary provider is how an infant begins to develop trust and to know that she is cared for and cared about.

Alice Honig says, "Loving touch is a secret ingredient that magically helps babies and young children feel emotionally secure. Offer caresses, back rubs and lap time freely" (2002). In her book on secure attachments, Honig encourages infant care providers to understand that establishing loving, trusting relationships with the babies in their care is essential. She suggests that it is easy for providers to think they should "keep a professional distance" from the families in their care. This, Honig says, is a misconception. "Love is the first ingredient of attachment," she claims. With increasing numbers of parents returning to the workplace shortly after giving birth, many infants will learn some of these lessons in love from their teachers.

Just how much a baby can and should be held is one of the issues to be negotiated between families and providers. Both parents and providers need to observe babies carefully in their earliest weeks of life and time in our care. Babies give us hints about their needs.

Paying attention to the wishes of individual families for their babies is also part of our job. In many cultures, babies are carried on their mothers' bodies at all times. For centuries, babies have been carried in wraps and slings while their parents go about their daily tasks. Every culture raises children successfully. Babies confined to cribs and playpens have grown up to be competent adults, just as have babies carried on their mothers' backs. There are also individual differences. Some babies prefer to be held all the time, while others have a less intense need. Some infants for a variety of reasons would just as soon not be touched. Our job is to try to figure out who needs what and when, and then to accommodate those needs.

Attachment Theory and Holding

In her writings, Magda Gerber is outspoken about the overuse of infant carriers. Adults believe that always holding the baby is good, she writes, just as previous generations believed that rarely holding the baby was good. She describes parents absentmindedly going about their work with an infant hung in a carrier, receiving very little of their focus, while the parents believe that mere body contact is enough (1998).

As I studied the literature on all of this, I kept thinking of the word *mindful*. It is clear that there are many approaches to caring for infants. Differences and temperament call for varied approaches to caring. Gerber is quick to suggest that truly focused attention is the most significant thing we can do for a little one. She also stresses that holding is good for babies, but so is being left alone for periods of time. Babies need to stretch and reach and feel their bodies. If they are always attached to a grown-up, their opportunities for growth are stifled.

Like so many other areas of child development, holding has undergone radical changes due to the negative impact of children not being held and cuddled enough in years past. Throughout the 1940s and '50s it was common practice to leave infants in cradles and playpens as long as they were fed, dry, and not crying too hard. Conventional wisdom held that picking a baby up without a specific reason would nurture an unnecessary need for adult attention. Gerber cautions us to strike a balance. She believes too many adults have been convinced that being loving means being constantly present and available to a baby. "To me, a mature, evolved person shows love by respecting the otherness of the beloved" (2003).

It is clear that there are many approaches to caring for infants. Differences and temperament call for varied approaches to caring.

Magda Gerber discusses the approach to infant caring in RIE centers, where teachers do not put pressure on themselves to pick up an infant the moment she cries. Instead, the teacher talks calmly and empathetically to the baby. "Yes, you are ready to eat now. Your time is coming. Right now I am feeding Jeremy, and when he's done, you and I will have our time together."

This approach is less hurried than that found in centers where teachers feel they must be all things to all babies all of the time. Giving oneself this impossible job description as either a parent or a provider can lead only to frustration, which the baby will feel as you hold her.

Certainly the elements of touch and holding are at the very heart of attachment theory. When Bowlby and Ainsworth pondered the development of babies, they initially looked at attachments broken by death or separation from the mother. It was when Harlow's research was published in 1958 that we took the giant step forward to seeing that the young need comfort as much as they need nourishment. Kennell and Klaus urge us to look to other cultures to see that Western culture has socially separated babies from their parents with inventions such as the baby carriage and nursery and that these may not be such advances after all. When Brazelton gave his *Infants and Mothers* (1983) the subtitle *Differences in Development,* it was a huge step forward for parents in this country—it was the beginning of individualizing our approaches, and it was the ending of keeping infants to arbitrary schedules for holding, feeding, and sleeping. It was the beginning of our comfort with the answer, "It depends!"

Today assessing development and responses to development have become subtle tools. We have learned that development depends on many things. When we assess what we know now about the importance to babies of touch and holding, we have many factors to base our choices on:

- Babies need to be held and touched.

- Holding helps an infant develop feelings of trust.

- Some babies have a greater need for and take more comfort in being held than others.

- Some parents and providers are able to be more accessible to infant demands than others.

- Decisions about holding or not should be based on observation and reflection as well as on feelings.

- How much you hold an infant depends on the baby, your beliefs, and your accessibility.

- These decisions should be made individually and not based on general principles about how much holding "ought" to be done.

Supporting Babies

Drawing from attachment theory, we can adapt a range of the ideas about how we hold and touch the babies in our care. Our decision depends on the baby's temperament, the parents' wishes and requests for their infant's care, the ratios in our infant rooms, our culture, and who we are. When Mary Ainsworth tried to duplicate her Uganda studies with infants and mothers in this country, she was delighted to find that some universal principles exist to guide us. These are the most important:

- Babies need and want to be held.

- Adults who are comfortable themselves are better able to comfort babies.

- We can best learn how much a baby wants to be held by careful observation.

(1967)

Babies Need and Want to Be Held
Erik Erikson taught us the importance of trust in an infant's first year of life. Holding a baby closely helps her develop trust. Holding lets her know we are there for her. Holding can sometimes sooth an infant's fretful crying or quiet a crying baby frightened by a loud noise. Holding can help us feel what a baby needs and help us know her better. Babies do not become demanding or fussy as a result of too much holding.

Comfortable Adults Make Better Comforters
When adults are comfortable with holding infants, infants enjoy being held. When adults have ambivalence about how much is too much or worry that they should let the baby cry it out, the baby

usually picks up on this stress and becomes more fretful. When teachers are tired, over ratios, or coming down with a cold, they can let the baby explore the world from a safe place on the floor. When parents are sleep deprived, they have difficulty cuddling babies in a relaxed way. Infant teachers can help parents by sharing this information. Most new parents need all the positive reassurance they can get. If parents are exhausted and you assure them that sometimes it really is okay to let the baby cry a bit while they take a breather, have a cup of tea, or regroup, you are not only helping the parent—you are also helping the baby.

Observation Is Key

If there is one thing that attachment theorists have in common, it is the conviction that we learn about attachment by watching babies. T. Berry Brazelton shows us that careful observation always guides us in our desire to know how much connection a baby wants and needs. Each infant is different. Desire for touch is a temperamental as well as a learned trait. If we watch the babies in our care carefully, we learn what they need from us and when. If we take the time to thoughtfully ponder Magda Gerber's RIE approach to infant caring, we can develop more confidence about our skills with babies and learn how to cope with the limitations our job creates for the babies in our care. Calm, reassuring conversation can reach out to one little one while we finish feeding another. We can delight in holding the babies whenever possible. We can delight in the fact that even little babies can learn that waiting is possible.

Supporting Families

Much of the discussion by current attachment theorists focuses on supporting families. Clearly the United States falls behind other industrialized nations in terms of helping new families deal with the complexities of balancing work and family life. Our field has been notable for its efforts to reach out to young families. Our current emphasis on understanding diversity and supporting families from many different circumstances is one of the positive influences of current research.

If there is a single message to help all of us bridge theory and practice for children and families, it is the constant reminder that there are many ways to successfully raise children. As we reach out to the families in our care, we can focus on three important points:

- Children survive and thrive in a variety of circumstances.

- Babies adapt to the schedules and routines their parents provide.

- Infant teachers and child care centers can be the source of support that extended families used to provide.

A Variety of Circumstances

When parents bring their very young children to us, they are often full of doubts and ambivalence. The United States has not kept up with the changes in family life over the last fifty years. The majority of all parents must work outside the home. Conventional wisdom continues to present an outdated twentieth-century model for caring for the young. We can support young families by assuring them that they are not alone in their struggle to balance work and family. Two-income parents and single-parent families have become the norm. We are their partners in raising the next generation. We can offer support, information, and a place to meet with others who are trying to raise their families in circumstances different from the ones in which they were raised. Our encouragement of young families is one of the greatest services we can provide.

Families may be stressed by bringing their babies into a child care center that is culturally different from their home—a different language spoken, different lullabies sung, different smells in the air, and most of all, different methods and beliefs about the basic needs of young babies present. It bears repeating that every culture raises babies successfully, even if their methods don't look like the ones we're used to. Our job is to adapt our program as much as possible to make it work for families.

Babies Will Adapt

Just as families in the early years of this country adapted to the conditions of the prairie and other new frontiers, the babies whose parents struggle today with jobs, commutes, and child care will also adapt. We are all trying to find our way. It is exciting to let families know that we can be their partners in rearing the next generation. Many of us work with families new to this country.

Chapter 7

Many things change with time, but the basic needs of babies and families are pretty constant. We can support refugee and immigrant families by respecting their unique needs. We can empathize with young families who struggle because they cannot live the same model of child rearing that worked for their parents. We all want happy, confident children, although we may have different ideas of how to get there. When the adults understand there are many ways of reaching the same end, children automatically feel safe and follow our lead.

The New Extended Family

It is a compliment to every infant center when parents say, "I feel so safe leaving my baby with you!" Child care centers can provide much of the support to young families once provided by extended families. It is not our goal to replace families, but with appropriate communication, flexibility, and support, we can work together to help today's children feel they have been raised within a family. We can offer the current wisdom on child rearing. We can recommend books and playthings for young children. We can listen. We can learn together. We can provide a structure that is not the same as extended families a century ago but that tries to provide an extended family's comforting benefits.

Dr. Spock reminds us that the answers to our questions of what to do with babies need to come from many places. We need to read, think, observe, reflect. We need to remember that no two children or situations are identical. We need to remember that when we make a decision and realize it wasn't the best one, we need to forgive ourselves and move on. Patterns developed over a lifetime make us who we are. No one ever went down the wrong road for life because of a single decision made in one moment about one action. Today the variety of publications, media presentations, and talk shows addressing raising children can feel overwhelming to those who care for infants and to parents. Finding one's own way takes time, reflection, and a comfort level that evolves over one's years of caring for children. Mindful parenting and teaching can help us all support the needs of families. Alice Honig says, "Most people associate parental love with easy solutions of holding, nursing, cuddling. What is much more difficult is to find the balance

94

between holding on and letting go. It is a lifelong struggle, and maybe the hardest part of parenting" (2002).

Discussion Questions

1. With your coworkers, create a list of positive reasons why a mother can feel comfortable with her decision to wean her infant before returning to work. Now make another list supporting a mother's choice to continue nursing upon returning to work. What considerations are involved with each decision?

2. What is your personal response to families sleeping in the same bed? How does that affect your work with families who let their babies cry it out in their own rooms? How does it affect your response to families who want their children to sleep together at the center during rest times? Can adaptations be made? Why or why not?

3. Anne Stonehouse suggests that we should keep certain "milestones" of development to ourselves rather than sharing with parents what they might be more pleased to discover on their own. What do you think of this perspective? Why?

Suggestions for Further Reading

Honig, Alice Sterling. 2002. *Secure relationships: Nurturing infant/toddler attachment in early care settings.* Washington, DC: National Association for the Education of Young Children.

Leach, Penelope. 1978. *Your baby and child: From birth to age five.* New York: Alfred A. Knopf.

Gandini, Lella, and Carolyn Pope Edwards, eds. 2001. *Bambini: The Italian approach to infant/toddler care.* New York: Teachers College Press.

Chapter 8: Infant Crying

A crying child makes adults dissolve.

—T. Berry Brazelton (1992)

Meeting the demands of a new baby who cries frequently is probably one of the first challenges for new parents. There are many reasons for this. Most new parents have little preparation for the task before them. The United States is doing a much better job than in decades past at providing classes for new parents. But, as Brazelton points out in *Touchpoints*, "Our present society does not adequately nurture and protect our new parents" (1992, 235). Many young couples still have a romantic view of newborns and family that leads them to be unrealistic about the constant demands of an infant. The human infant is totally dependent for a long period of time. This situation is complicated by the fact that sleep deprivation, well-wishers, and role changes all hit the new parents at once. New parents who expected to feel whole and fulfilled by giving birth are shocked to find themselves exhausted and exasperated instead.

It can be a very heavy burden for new parents to grapple with the reality and demands of raising a child, especially if they thought it would be easy compared to being an MBA or an attorney. Many of the young mothers I talk to find it humbling to admit what a huge challenge it is to be attuned to a newborn. It is a struggle even for people whose lives include a fair amount of stability and support. For people who are very young, poor, depressed, or socially isolated, it can be overwhelming.

The early childhood field has done much to encourage infant care providers to be supportive and nonjudgmental with new parents. It has been my observation over the years, however, that we are better at talking about this than actually doing it. I think there are three reasons for this.

- The lack of infant-specific child care training

- A failure to reflect on the extent to which our own family's notions of what is best for babies affects our practice as infant teachers

- Inadequate infrastructures to support the stresses of working in an infant room

In order for infant teachers to do a fine job of supporting parents stressed by infant crying and inadequate responses, several things need to be in place. Early childhood courses in infant care are a must. Information about how best to support babies and their parents in the earliest weeks and months of life has expanded, enriching our professional resources. Using these resources rather than relying on our grandmother's ideas is essential. Professional development resources must continue to be created by the field, because infant teachers need a lot of support.

Just as elementary education is an inadequate background for preschool teachers, preschool and kindergarten training is inadequate preparation for being an infant teacher. All over the country, infant teachers are caring for babies without ever taking an infant development course. This needs to change. If you are an infant teacher without academic training in infant-toddler development, look for resources to learn more. You would not expect to act as a defense attorney in court if you had never been to law school. Experience as a spectacular kindergarten teacher does not adequately prepare you to be a spectacular infant teacher.

All of us are vulnerable to the impact of our families of origin. Don't discount the power of those old scripts in shaping how you believe you should respond to the babies in your care. Upon reflection, you may be surprised to see how much you do at work based on what your own family culture thought was appropriate. Your work with babies and their families in an infant program should be based on current understanding of sensible approaches to infant care, combined with ongoing support for and collaboration with the babies' families.

Some experts in early childhood believe that we should always do some form of looping—that is, moving with a group of children as they grow—in early education programs. One of the many reasons for this belief is that it prevents teachers from burning out as a result of the excessive crying of infants, the search for autonomy of two-year-olds, or the intense enthusiasm four-year-olds bring to their days. If we change the ages we work with every few years, we keep current in child development for all of the early years and avoid getting too much of the downside in every age.

It is important for infant teachers to understand how stressful it is to spend an entire day with a baby who is fretful. There is much in print to remind new parents that it is normal to feel overwhelmed or even angry at a brand-new baby who cries and cries. This applies to infant teachers as well. Our response to the baby must be nurturing, sensitive, and supportive. Similarly, our response to our own feelings should be responsive as well. Being an infant teacher is a rewarding but also demanding and sometimes exhausting position.

Attachment Theory and Infant Crying

Several points by the primary attachment theorists affect our practices in response to crying today. John Bowlby and René Spitz discuss the rage and loneliness an infant feels when his cries are ignored. They try to raise the consciousness of the psychoanalytic community to the fact that when an infant stops trying to get attention (by crying), he has given up hope that he has the power to get his needs met. We can apply Bowlby and Spitz's observation by stressing to infant teachers that an infant who never cries may not be fine. We need to carefully observe and make constant assessments of the babies in our care.

Mary Ainsworth, after observing babies and mothers in this country and cross-culturally, determines that mothers who are comfortable and supportive of their infants' cries have babies who cry less than mothers who have multiple challenges (for example, poverty, mental illness, sleep deprivation). These very

Babies need caregivers to support parents as much as they need caregivers to care for them.

challenged mothers are more stressed and less responsive to their babies' crying. We apply Ainsworth's work when we support the babies in our care by supporting their parents. Babies need their parents to be as relaxed and comfortable as possible so they can give the babies the care and attention they need. Babies need caregivers to support parents as much as they need caregivers to care for them.

Brazelton, Spock, and Gerber challenge us to be balanced. We need to be careful observers of the babies in our care, reflect on the biases we bring to our work, and work cooperatively with parents to determine what is best for their infants. Brazelton's emphasis on differences in infant development is a gift to all those who live and work with babies. Sharing that information with parents can help them develop confidence in their parenting abilities. Little feels worse than being the parent of a fussy baby who is up half the night when your sister-in-law has a baby the same age who sleeps peacefully both day and night.

Brazelton points out that babies come in several temperamental varieties, and parents don't get to select the temperament they prefer. One of the serious impacts of the baby's temperament is that it shapes the parents' image of the child and influences their adjustment to the style of their infant (1992). It is easier to be a parent to an easy baby than it is to be a parent to a difficult one. This is not fair. It is hard. Information can help families cope with excessive crying and other traits of the more challenging infant. Even child care providers often think the parents of the easy baby are good parents and wonder where the parents of the fussy baby are going wrong. It is a very common occurrence in infant care centers, and something we all have to guard against. Such judgment has a detrimental effect on the self-esteem of the fussy baby's parents, even if the judgment is never spoken. Instead, infant teachers can support families by providing helpful information about differences in temperament.

We must also look more carefully at excessive infant crying than we have been inclined to do in decades past. For a long time, infant crying was quickly termed colic and considered typical of most new infants. To some extent this is true. Reviews of the literature indicate that in many situations, intense infant crying in the first weeks and months has no long-term effect (Zero to Three 2008). Studies also indicated that when a number of variables coexist, such as maternal depression, lack of financial or human resources, and limited support or coping strategies, excessive infant crying can lead to a decline in emotional connection between the infant and the parent. It is only when excessive crying goes on for many weeks or when parents do not have coping strategies that normal crying may become atypical and an indicator of risk for later psycho-social challenges. When discussing infant crying, it is critical to look at the circumstances of the crying baby and the effect his crying has on his relationship with his family. A lot of crying is merely colic and will pass without leaving challenging traces. But we know now that this is not always the case.

In *Touchpoints*, T. Berry Brazelton documents that 85 percent of infants routinely go through a fussy period at the end of the day. This is the typical and usually benign crying I've described above. Brazelton explains the infant crying from a baby's perspective to new parents. He says babies have to unwind after a long day, just like the rest of us. He refers to colic as letting off steam. This is helpful information to new parents, since it normalizes the behavior and gives them one less thing to worry about. When parents can cope with the actual behavior without worrying about the baby's well-being, it is easier for parents, and thus the young family, to stay on track. Parents who worry excessively about a baby's crying tend to reinforce it. Usually when colic is developmental, it goes away by about the third month of life.

Some of the questions surrounding infant crying are fairly easy to answer, although it may not seem so to new parents if they have several friends and family members giving them conflicting advice. Usually parents want to know how quickly they should respond. Unfortunately, many extended family members still believe that responding too quickly to infant tears places parents at risk of raising a demanding tyrant. Even Benjamin Spock admonished, "If she continues to give in, he realizes after a while that he has his poor tired mother under his thumb and he becomes increasingly disagreeable and tyrannical in demanding this service" (1970). This was spoken of a three-month-old infant!

Fortunately, today most parents report that they have been to some kind of parent preparation class before giving birth. Infant crying is always high on the agenda and is usually presented as the first form of communication available to a new baby. It is no longer viewed as manipulative but rather the only way babies have to alert us to their hunger, fatigue, fear, or discomfort. Parents are expected to respond quickly and consistently to their infant's tears. We know that babies who are responded to consistently begin to develop trust in the adults in their world. We also know that they begin to feel competent in their own ability to get their needs met by signaling their distress to their caregivers.

Supporting Babies

Infant crying can be just as taxing for infant care providers as it is for new parents, especially when one sensitive baby sets off a whole infant group. Here are some ways to help infants who cry more than usual:

- Take care not to overstimulate the baby.

- Limit your comforting strategies.

- Swaddle the baby for comfort (wrap her arms next to her body and her legs in a soft blanket).

- Limit the baby's contact and interaction with strangers at child care.

- Watch the baby carefully for signs of what works.

- Refuse to let your esteem as a provider be affected. The baby's crying is probably not connected to problems at child care (or at home).

Let's take these one at a time.

During the 1960s there was an emphasis stressed by both educators and pediatric practitioners on the need to stimulate the newborn in order to nurture cognitive development. We know now that too much stimulation can be detrimental. For this reason, it's important to keep the infant room calm. Pale, warm colors, quiet, and softness should predominate. Music should be kept low and not played continually. Watching carefully for children's individual capacity for stimulation is also helpful. Brazelton tells us that babies actually turn away from us when they have had all the contact they are interested in for a time (1988).

Another way to keep the environment calm is to limit your comforting strategies. Don't rock, sing, *and* turn out the lights all at once—try one at a time. Magda Gerber repeats a simple but sound piece of advice to parents and providers of care to young babies: "Slow down!" Listening to a screaming baby is hard on everyone, including the baby. Infant teachers should not allow themselves to become frantic, going from one comforting strategy to the next in an anxiety-ridden attempt to calm the baby down now. Little ones need time to be able to transition comfortably. Instead, try one strategy and wait for it to make a positive change. If after a period of time (which will differ with each baby, but try at least ten or fifteen minutes) you don't get results, then try something else. Remember that babies can feel your stress, and racing about to force results only makes a baby's fretfulness worse.

The technique of swaddling, another way of reducing stimulation, comes from ancient times and many cultures but has only recently been rediscovered in the United States. In the infant room, we frequently see a baby's startle reflex—that sudden physical reflex which causes the baby's arms or legs to move quickly and involuntarily. This can startle or frighten the baby. Swaddling helps with this, as well as with general overstimulation. Wrap the baby firmly in a warm, soft blanket. Some babies are comforted and feel great security from this simple adjustment. Others feel confined. As with all strategies suggested here, swaddling depends on the baby.

All infant teachers need to be aware of the limited tolerance new babies have for a continually changing cast of characters in their lives. Babies are not oblivious to strangers in their midst. If your environment can be arranged in a way that offers strangers the opportunity to check with an adult before bursting into the space where babies are playing, it benefits everyone.

I always enjoy observing successful teachers when they settle children for rest times. I am awed as the infant teachers move from baby to baby, rubbing this one's back, patting that one's head, holding one finger of a third baby till she nods off. Just as with determining the needs of older children, a key to successful strategies for working with newborns is careful observation. If a caregiver watches, she soon learns who enjoys the sun, who needs to be in the shade, who seems to love soft music, who prefers quiet.

If a caregiver watches, she soon learns who enjoys the sun, who needs to be in the shade, who seems to love soft music, who prefers quiet.

Infant teachers need to remind one another that crying is a baby's means of communicating. It is not a signal that something is wrong. If you view these periods of crying as an opportunity to learn more about the babies in your care, you will feel more successful. Remind yourself that fussy babies are not trying to be troublesome—they simply don't know yet what makes them comfortable, and they are trying to figure it out. One of the most important bits of information we have received from recent advances in infant research is that babies cry when they are lonely or bored. They are not spoiled—they are trying to connect.

Supporting Parents

Initially the idea of answering a baby's cries quickly and consistently sounds the reasonable and the appropriate choice to new parents. When attending childbirth classes, participants often enthusiastically denounce any form of punitive response to their children. Often they vow never to yell, spank, swear, or otherwise engage in the inappropriate methods their parents were sometimes guilty of using. This, of course, is before the baby has thrown up repeatedly in the new car or the new mother has tried on even her fat jeans and been unable to zip them up. It's before weeks of sleep deprivation and advice from friends and parenting gurus and mothers and mothers-in-law and aunties who have never even given birth. It's different after all of the casseroles lovingly prepared by well-wishers are gone and the only milk in the house with a current use-by date is breast milk. Then the going gets rough! Then the baby books' encouraging calm approaches have an empty ring. This is when young families need T. Berry Brazelton in residence.

It is hurtful to young parents to experience having their feelings of helplessness or frustration from their baby's excessive crying dismissed by important people in their lives. New parents are already feeling the stress of transition to a new way of life. They are frequently sleep deprived. They need empathy and acknowledgment that dealing with an extremely fussy baby is exhausting. Infant teachers also need this understanding. I have been in programs where tired toddler teachers act as if infant teachers have an easy job because the children in their care are not mobile. Increased empathy improves life for all of us!

All new parents experience stress in the transition to parenthood, particularly first-time parents. But the families of babies who cry excessively are sometimes at risk in a way that those with calmer infants are not, for they often find the transition to parenting more difficult and stressful. They are likely to experience more judgment from family members, friends, and even strangers about their child's sensitivity. Thus they need special support from child care providers.

We know that positive attachments in the early weeks and months of life lead to positive parent-child relationships, positive social relationships with others, and a blueprint for intimate relationships for the rest of a baby's life. Therefore much is at stake. Child care providers have a vested interest in nurturing the most positive of relationships for all of the babies and parents in our country. You can nurture these relationships by earning a PhD in infant development or by smiling pleasantly at the young couple whose baby just screamed all afternoon in the infant room and saying sympathetically, "What a little trooper. He must be so tired. It will be good for all of us when he outgrows this fussy period."

When you want to help parents, you can try some of these techniques:

- Remind them that many of us did this as infants—and turned out okay.

- Remind them that it is easier for babies to relax with people who are not themselves exhausted and stressed out.

- Remind them that Brazelton says 85 percent of babies go through this.

- Let them know that frustration is an appropriate response to exhaustion and that giving up the dream of the Gerber baby isn't easy.

- Remind them that continuous overload makes all of us feel powerless, but they are not failures because the baby can't settle.

The most important thing you can do to support parents whose babies are crying a lot is to help them remember that their babies are normal and that they are fine parents. It is easy for them to believe this is the only baby who has ever cried and cried! Tell stories to your parent group about babies in past years who struggled with excessive crying and then grew into peaceful little people.

Help parents remember that it's easier for babies to rest in unexhausted arms—which might explain the baby's tendency not to cry when Grandma or the provider holds her. Other adults who can soothe the baby didn't just give birth and they are probably not staying up all night with a fussy baby. These are points that can't be emphasized enough. It is demoralizing for new parents to try everything they know how to do to comfort a baby who continues to wail. These exhausted individuals need constant reminders that they are doing all the right things and that the baby can't help it. It's also critical to remind them that the fact that the baby stops crying when someone else takes over is not an indication that they are not good at comforting—only that their exhaustion and frustration are being felt by the baby, who is also exhausted and frustrated.

It is important for parents to understand how common it is for babies to have fussy periods and to go through patches when they are fussier than usual. Brazelton's 85 percent figure is enormously reassuring to parents. Most infant teachers are unaware of Brazelton's statistics. For infant teachers or parents who have walked, rocked, and sung all day only to be met by more tears, it is crucial to remember that crying is typical for the majority of newborns.

Years ago, I remember a professor of mine using the words "fleeting fantasies of violence" to describe the feelings of adults who have spent hours trying to comfort a screaming infant with no success. Both infant teachers and new parents need to remember that these feelings seem earned, given the situation, and are nothing to be ashamed of. In the moment, the best solution may be to take a break and let someone else take over. In the long run, grappling with separating the Gerber baby myths from the reality of caring for newborns is the only solution. It isn't easy to give up the fantasies of perfect babies, especially if all you ever wanted was to be an early educator or a parent.

Infant teachers need to remind parents as well as one another that caring for a fretful baby is exhausting and stressful. Help parents and each other by remembering that babies have only crying as a means of communication, that they have no idea what is making them cry, and that abandoning them to cry it out is usually only going to add to their pain as they struggle alone.

Infant teachers can also help parents and their fussy infants connect despite the infants' distress. In fact, fostering this relationship is one of the most important things you can do. Use these techniques to help infants and parents connect:

- Share everything you know about the vicious cycle of crying, tense reaction on the part of parents, and more excessive crying.

- Point out every positive relational characteristic you can observe, no matter how small.

- Help parents understand the factors that may make it easier for a baby to settle at child care.

- Encourage family and friends to give stress-alleviating gifts to the new family. Pizza delivery, full-body massage for the mother, diaper service for six weeks—all will help more than that adorable outfit the baby doesn't need anyway.

- Suggest professional supports (lactation experts, pediatric counselors, postpartum depression experts) as a way to get a positive foundation in place.

Many parents just don't have enough experience with babies to notice the important ways their baby is connecting with them or is soothed by their presence. It is such an easy thing to compliment parents on the job they do with their children. Try telling parents the many ways they support their child's growth and development. Especially when we care for infants with difficult temperaments, it is essential to look for every sincere compliment we can offer to a parent—perhaps something like, "See how she looks at you? We haven't seen a smile like that all day." Just a few words spoken in support of the baby-parent relationship can send a family home at the end of the day feeling hopeful or successful.

It is often the case that infants and even older children are easier for teachers than for parents. This can be a terrible blow to parents' self-esteem. It is part of our job description as early educators to empower families to be all that they can be. It is important when working with families to remind them that when they bring their children to the center, the children become the exclusive focus of their teachers. We are not also trying to do yard work, shovel snow, pay bills, or do laundry. We have the luxury of early childhood-specific educations and jobs that allow us to focus entirely on the children in our care. We have an environment designed to be interesting to babies and children—and the most interesting attraction of all—other babies! We work with babies during the day in a relatively stable routine, while parents see them at the beginning and end of the day, when the whole family is transitioning from sleeping to working and back again. Parents do not experience our luxuries. Help them by pointing out these facts and by expressing your respect for their serious work in raising children.

We are finally beginning to acknowledge what a huge responsibility it is to bring an infant into the world. We are beginning to see that baby showers often deliver gifts in quantities that families don't really need. What do families really need? Help! Meals for a week help. Child care or special trips for the siblings helps. Disposable diapers or a diaper service helps. Telling new parents how we struggled when we were new parents helps too. Letting families know that they are not alone always helps.

When young families live far away from extended family, professional supports become increasingly important. As early educators, we can help families know that it is often challenging to establish a nursing routine. It is challenging to deal daily with a temperamentally challenging little one. It is always a surprise to reconcile the reality of parenting with the myths or media images of having a baby. Sometimes help from professionals can ease the burden.

Research suggests that counseling in the early months can make a substantial difference in positive outcomes for the whole family when excessive crying has plagued the peace, sleep environment, and domestic tranquillity of a family for several months. Parent groups can be helpful to young families because sharing with others can remove some of the feelings of isolation. Studies indicate, however, that these support groups are not as beneficial to the family group as pediatric psychologists. Normalizing the idea of professional intervention is an enormous gift to young families struggling with excessive crying or other challenges to the parent-infant relationship. This is another topic where a sensitively shared personal story can make a big difference. For example, tell the parents you wish you had taken your four-year-old for play therapy a long time ago and that it has made such a difference in family life since he has been going (Zero to Three 2008).

As with most of the issues surrounding infant care, there are many different choices one can make regarding response to infant crying. Most books for young parents today urge them to give themselves a break. One of the things we know about attachment formation between babies and parents is that mutual delight helps attachment occur. Most experts encourage parents to watch and listen to their babies and to progress in the way that makes this particular family feel comfortable. In the 1970s, Penelope Leach encouraged young parents to focus entirely on their newborn and let cooking, cleaning, accounting, and other tasks be put on hold while parents and infants come together as a family. This is still good advice. We know it is easier for a parent to relate well to her newborn if the parent is rested. If the parent accepts that her baby is temperamentally challenging, then the parent can develop coping strategies to help her infant through the long process of developing self-regulation. Whether the parents always respond in the same way is not as essential if, most of the time, parents are comfortable with the road they are taking with their baby.

It is in the best interest of babies and their parents to believe that excessive crying in infancy will pass and not bring later developmental or emotional challenges. It is important for pediatricians, child care providers, infant teachers, and family members to offer maximal support to new families. It is also important professionally and personally for all of us to remember that patterns create meaning in terms of family life, development, and risk. Economic challenges, coupled with isolation, lack of available supports, and developmental challenges (for example, feeding, growth, sleep, and excessive crying) place infants and their families at risk of damaged attachments. Paying attention to these multiple factors, doing what we can to lessen their impact, and providing support to young families will strengthen the development of individual babies and their families as well as our collective lives on a small planet. The next

It is part of our job description as early educators to empower families to be all that they can be.

time you're on a plane with a screaming infant, instead of offering a cold stare, reach out and comfort the parent. Tell a story. Offer encouragement. Smile. The healing effect that acceptance and support offer to young families as they try to transition to parenting is amazing. It is both the joy and the responsibility of early educators to help the families of the babies we care for.

Discussion Questions

1. Have you ever reflected on connections between what your family thought was an appropriate response to infant crying and how you respond to infants who cry frequently? What are those connections?

2. How much do you think the "conventional wisdom" that picking up crying infants creates demanding babies has affected your behavior as an infant teacher?

3. When you are working with babies who cry frequently, at what point do you decide that the crying is excessive and may need pediatric intervention? Then what do you do?

Suggestions for Further Reading

Papousek, M., M. Schieche, and H. Wurmser. 2008. *Disorders of behavioral and emotional regulation in the first years of life: Early risks and intervention in the developing parent-infant relationship.* Washington, DC: Zero to Three.

Halfon, Neal, Kathryn Taaffe McLearn, and Mark A. Schuster, eds. 2002. *Child rearing in America: Challenges facing parents with young children.* New York: Cambridge University Press.

Greenman, Jim, Anne Stonehouse, and Gigi Schweikert. 2008. *Prime times.* St. Paul, MN: Redleaf Press.

Chapter 9: Separation and Stranger Anxiety

Virtually all normal infants develop special attachments to the people who care for them, and some infants are more secure in their attachments than others.

—Mary Ainsworth (1967)

Newborns recognize their parents and other special people in their lives very early. But they are not extremely discriminating in those first few weeks and months of life about who keeps them snuggled, warm, fed, changed, and comfy. This discrimination occurs somewhere between six and fourteen months of age, depending on the particular infant. At this time, they begin to experience both separation and stranger anxiety. Separation anxiety is the upset an infant feels when he is not in the presence of his most important people. Stranger anxiety is the upset he feels when an unrecognized adult enters his space. Both concepts are important to the work of infant teachers. How we handle stranger anxiety and separation anxiety among the babies in our care and their families determines, at least to some extent, the success of babies in developing secure attachments during their first year of life.

Attachment Theory and Separation

We know from both Bowlby and Erikson that one of the earliest developmental tasks is learning to trust and feel attached to significant people. Casual observation tends to indicate that although infants do show almost an immediate preference for some people (parents, primary caregivers, older siblings, aunties), in the early weeks and months of life it is not difficult to pass a baby around a room of friends or relatives without creating unusual distress in the baby. Somewhere between six and fourteen months of age, however, we note a dramatic change in the reaction of infants to strangers or to separation from significant people.

111

We usually connect this reaction, at least in part, to the concept of *object permanence* described by the Swiss psychologist Jean Piaget. Piaget defines object permanence as the baby coming to understand that something exists even when she can't see it (1976). Suddenly the baby is aware that her father or her primary caregiver comes and goes and that when he or she is not here, he or she is somewhere else. Then the baby develops the sense that crying can sometimes bring the special person back.

Alice Honig gives a clear definition of the stage: "Separation anxiety is evidenced by a baby's increased anxiety and fear in meeting new people and entering new situations as well as by his intensified clinging behavior. Clinging and crying upon separation from a parent or familiar caregiver is normal during this period. These behaviors reflect the child's attachment" (2002). I suggest that infant teachers share this definition in writing at a conference with each baby's parents or as part of an orientation to infant care services. Like biting during toddlerhood, this is an issue better handled *before* it happens.

The differences between *separation anxiety* and *stranger anxiety* are very slight. Both are related to the baby's growing attachment to the important people in her life. *Separation anxiety* refers to the baby's negative reaction to the absence or departure of her primary caregivers. *Stranger anxiety* refers to the baby's negative reaction to the presence or arrival of people she doesn't know. Reactions to separation or to strangers are as varied as personalities. Temperament usually affects the intensity of reaction. Some babies whimper, while others wail.

Similarly, parents react in many different ways when their babies begin to go through separation anxiety. Brazelton reminds us that parents experience grief and loss when they first bring their baby to any form of out-of-home care (1998). Because parents are usually not totally prepared for how much they love their baby, they are sometimes surprised by the grief, guilt, and even anger they feel. Brazelton suggests that parents often depend on a variety of defense

Often just expressing the feelings out loud and discussing them can help lessen their intensity. When parents become more comfortable, they and the baby usually experience an easing of separation behaviors.

mechanisms to help them make it through this difficult and poignant transition; the three most common are denial, projection, and detachment.

It is important to note that these feelings are frequently unconscious. Brazelton tries to gently point out the feelings to parents and to support them in developing coping strategies. Often just expressing the feelings out loud and discussing them can help lessen their intensity. When parents become more comfortable, they and the baby usually experience an easing of separation behaviors.

Very frequently, parents' defense mechanisms are interpreted literally by child care providers, who decide the parents are cold and indifferent to their infant. Rather than recognizing the defense mechanisms for what they are—a means of surviving a distressing passage for young parents—caregivers react with judgment. It is at times like these that caregivers are at risk for developing the so-called savior complex, believing that their job is to rescue the baby emotionally from uncaring parents, which can only hurt the baby, parents, and child care provider.

Supporting Babies

There are several ways we can support babies through these very typical stages of development. Brazelton's work in *Touchpoints* (1992) can be an essential reference for infant teachers. When caregivers know and anticipate typical stages of development, they can share the information with the parents. Then, as partners, teachers and parents can work to support the baby. Supporting infants (and their parents) through this somewhat trying stage of development is easier if you use these techniques:

- Provide brief written information about separation and stranger anxiety before they surface.

- Work with parents to agree on routines for saying good-bye.

- Determine the best approach to helping each baby through stranger and separation anxiety.

- Establish infant room policies about strangers that are supportive of infants in this stage.

113

Information for Parents

When we give parents an alert to coming changes in their baby's behaviors, we are helping them better navigate this new developmental stage. All attachment research points to the delicate interconnections between parent and infant behavior. If parents are surprised or alarmed by sudden changes in their baby's behaviors, they can become unsettled, and unsettling parental behavior usually results in unsettling infant behavior. Just as information about typical toddler biting does not prevent biting from happening, knowing about stranger or separation anxiety cannot prevent either from occurring. Both are part of a typical and anticipated stage of development. But when we are able to warn parents, they are prepared and more relaxed and can ease the stress of their baby rather than adding to it.

This is where Brazelton's Touchpoints approach can be so helpful. If infant teachers take time before the baby reaches six months to prepare parents for this typical behavior, parents are less likely to be surprised or dismayed by the sudden change in their baby's behavior. Most of us are better able to cope with difficult circumstances when we know they are coming—we can say, "Oh my! Here it comes." Parents and teachers can plan together about how to handle separation during this phase. This does not mean it will be easy to endure the baby's tears and clinging, but knowing that this behavior is typical and will end, that the baby loves her parents and doesn't want to be separated from them, takes some of the sting out of the situation for everyone.

Saying Good-bye

It is easiest to develop a plan with families for saying good-bye before good-byes become emotionally difficult. While parents may not completely understand the need for consistency before their babies enter the separation anxiety phase, if they understand how much easier it will make separation for them and for their baby later on, they are usually willing to work with teachers on a plan. This procedure for supporting babies really has two parts.

First, caregivers determine with the family how they would like to deal with partings. Caregivers encourage parents not to sneak away and explain to them how much harder this can make the separation in the long run, when their baby is afraid that if she takes her attention off them, they may disappear at any moment. Just as you have learned to be honest with the three-year-old who is afraid to go to the doctor and get a shot by saying something like, "It will hurt, but only for a minute," you need to be honest with parents. Trying to make it easier on yourself or parents by having Mom or Grandpa slip away without a good-bye only prolongs the agony. Changing care arrangements is also likely to make things worse— better to wait a few months.

Second, caregivers agree to take the baby gently from the parent (even while she clings to her parent and screams). Then, when the parent has gone, caregivers accept the responsibility to give this little one the special attention she needs while she wails from the loss of her family member.

Individual Approaches

As with so many other areas of our work as early educators, observation can really help us help babies at this difficult transition in their development. We may want to spend extra time holding, rocking, or stroking a crying infant whose father has just left. Or we may notice that this baby prefers to be distracted by a favorite book or toy. Another baby may just need a good cry and will then find his own way to settle himself after Nana's departure. The important thing is to observe the child and follow his cues to find what works best to acknowledge his feelings and settle him into the program. It's also critical for all infant teachers to understand how hard this painful transition is for both baby and parent and to provide the extra patience, nurturance, and support that help everyone survive this phase.

Infant Room Practices

Since we know that separation and stranger anxiety are such common but difficult stages in early infancy, it only makes sense to establish center policies that support babies at this period and that support those who care for them. If the infant program is part of a larger preschool and child care program, it is particularly important for directors to support their teachers with a stranger-free environment policy. If a typical infant room has eight babies and two teachers, and a "stranger" (who could be a preschool teacher from two classrooms down) walks in to see if teachers are going to the conference next weekend, she may leave two screaming babies in her wake. Then teachers are busy with only two of their six for the next twenty minutes, when the whole situation could easily have been avoided.

When we plan ahead, talk with parents about coming developmental changes, and remind our colleagues of essential policies for a comfortable infant room, we do a great deal to help the babies in our care develop secure attachments with all of the significant adults in their lives.

Supporting Parents

Separation anxiety offers competent infant caregivers the opportunity to strengthen the family unit by explaining how these fits of wailing at separation or reunion are really an indication that all is well between parents and baby. Babies, and older children, too, reserve their best and worst reactions for their parents because of the passionate connections between families and children. The problem is that the new experience of being a parent is so huge and so overwhelming that often parents don't realize what is going on.

Brazelton encourages infant care providers to understand that separation is first a challenge for parents. There is a huge and painful emotion when babies first start in care. Then, once babies achieve object permanence and start missing their parents, the baby's challenge also becomes one of emotional intensity. This makes it a family challenge because the interactions between the baby and her parents will diminish or increase the problem with time. Child care settings are the modern extended family. As part of that extended family, we can help mediate the pain of infants and parents by helping them navigate this very typical but also deeply emotional part of life.

Child care providers can help parents through separation anxiety using these suggestions:

- Don't take parents' concerns personally.

- Offer parents articles about typical development.

- Give parents lots of positive feedback.

Take Parents' Concerns Calmly

It is a balancing act for infant teachers to offer the babies in their care large doses of love and nurturance and the parents matter-of-fact receptiveness when they express concerns that can sometimes feel like criticism. It is human to feel hurt. It is professional to realize this concern has nothing to do with the quality of care we are providing. It is important to remember that parents need defense mechanisms to transition through difficult stages with their little ones. If caregivers have done their homework and are prepared to help parents anticipate changes in their baby's behaviors, they experience less parental concern. Still, it is hard for parents to walk away from a clinging, crying infant, and predictable, even understandable, that parents sometimes look at the caregiver or at the program, convinced that something must be wrong when their child is so upset. Of course they ask, "What does all this mean?" And of course parents sometimes have legitimate questions or concerns about the program or valuable suggestions about how things might be done better for them or their children. It can be a huge challenge to sort out when to offer emotional support to parents who are alarmed by their child's separation anxiety and when to question your own policies or the way you are handling separation with a particular child. As always, listening and asking questions are key. It is hard for caregivers not to take criticism or questioning personally, but it is what the position demands.

Talking about separation anxiety also gives infant teachers an excellent opportunity to stress to new parents how important they are in their baby's life. When caregivers share affirmations with parents about their strengths and expertise with the new baby, parents become more relaxed and confident. The less anxiety parents feel about their skill at caring well for their little one, the better they will be at caring for him.

Offer Articles to Support Parents

Written material can also help parents support their babies by respecting infants' sudden and seemingly inexplicable desire to stay close to their primary people. An article can help a parent explain calmly to Auntie Sarah that the baby is going through a stage of wanting to stay pretty close to Dad or Grandma right now and encourage friends and relatives not to take it personally. Articles about development can support parents and empower them to be sensitive to their infant's needs at this delicate stage and remind them how typical and transitory this behavior is.

When parents know about object permanence and stranger and separation anxiety, they are not as likely to make significant changes to their baby's routines at this vulnerable stage of development. Articles that stress differences in development are also very helpful to parents. Some babies experience little or no obvious separation anxiety, while others are painfully distressed for weeks. Parents tend to take physical differences in stride more easily. They don't say, "Oh no, my baby is taller than his cousin!" When they leave a little one at Grandma's for an evening with his cousin of the same age and he wails for a good part of the evening, the parent often feels inadequate. Caregivers can help by providing articles that stress the typical differences in development and temperament—things parents often haven't been told about. Many parents absorb information differently from reading articles than from talking with a caregiver in the middle of the infant room while they are saying good-bye to or being reunited with their babies. Offering them material to read gives them one more way to learn.

Give Positive Feedback

It is easy for infant teachers to forget that parents don't have the same academic background in child development that is part of an early educator's toolbox. Knowing that parents experience anxiety when their babies experience anxiety, caregivers can help by continually reminding parents that this clinging behavior and tearfulness is a compliment to the parent-child relationship. You can share positive stories, tell parents what seems to be working for you at child care, and ask for their advice about how best to meet their baby's needs. Sometimes teachers forget to get back to parents who have offered a suggestion. A simple "I tried that cheek stroking technique you suggested, and she calmed down right away!" can help parents feel competent and knowledgeable about their baby's needs.

In summary, when babies have been in care for several months, the sudden change in behavior that goes with separation anxiety or stranger anxiety can be unsettling for parents as well as for caregivers. Several teachers have shared stories with me about parents' fear of wrongdoing at the center after a baby who has happily transitioned for months suddenly starts screaming and clinging upon separation. It makes sense that if parents have not heard about this typical stage of development, they may be very upset and frightened by the sudden and intense change in their baby's reaction to being left at child care. Infant teachers can prevent this frightening experience by talking with parents in advance. If the opportunity to prepare parents has already passed, then providers can make the most of a difficult situation by not interpreting the parents' concern as an insult. Don't take it personally. Parents' fear and anxiety as well as caution or even blame are pretty common and understandable responses to this behavior if they don't see it coming.

Knowing that parents experience anxiety when their babies experience anxiety, caregivers can help by continually reminding parents that this clinging behavior and tearfulness is a compliment to the parent-child relationship.

The key to negotiating this developmental passage is positive and continual communication between parents and providers. When caregivers and parents talk openly with each other about their desire to make these transitions easier on the baby, when they share their fears about appropriately meeting one another's needs in this parent-provider partnership, everyone can come closer to facing this initial separation with understanding and courage. A positive first experience with separation anxiety helps everyone—babies, parents, and caregivers—deal with what Judith Viorst calls the "necessary losses" that are a continual part of the human experience (1998).

Discussion Questions

1. Last week you talked to Heather, a mom in your program, whose nine-month-old has started screaming every morning when Heather leaves. You told her it means that the baby loves her and is sad when she leaves. Today Sara, another mother in your program and a good friend of Heather, comes in worried because her eleven-month-old has never cried at separation. She is afraid she and her child are not securely attached. How do you respond?

2. Think about the families of babies in your care. Can you recall times when they demonstrated the common defense mechanisms described by T. Berry Brazelton? What were their behaviors? How did you respond?

3. Do you struggle with center personnel entering your room unannounced and creating tearful "stranger anxiety" scenes? What policies could you put in place to avoid such happenings?

Suggestions for Further Reading

Hast, Fran, and Ann Hollyfield. 1999. *Infant and toddler experiences.* St. Paul, MN: Redleaf Press.

Karr-Morse, Robin, and Meredith S. Wiley. 1997. *Ghosts from the nursery: Tracing the roots of violence.* New York: The Atlantic Monthly Press.

Karen, Robert. 1998. *Becoming attached: First relationships and how they shape our capacity to love.* New York: Oxford University Press.

Chapter 10: Competence and Confidence

[Attachment] refers to the dimension of the infant care-giver relationship involving protection and security regulation. Within this theoretic framework, attachment is conceptualized as an intense and enduring affectional bond that the infant develops with the mother figure, a bond that is biologically rooted in the function of protection from danger.

—John Bowlby, 1982

By closely supervising our infants, by allowing them to do what they are capable of, by restraining ourselves from rescuing them too often, by waiting and waiting and waiting, by giving minimal help when they really need it, we allow our infants to learn and grow at their own time and in their own way. I believe that, no matter how much and how fast the world changes, a well-grounded, competent, and confident person is best equipped to adapt to it. This is our goal.

—Magda Gerber, 1998

How do competence and confidence connect with attachment theory? John Bowlby's definition of attachment above provides the answer. Consider the words "biologically rooted in the function of protection from danger"—Bowlby is saying that the bond of attachment is connected to the baby's feeling of safety and protection.

When a baby experiences a secure attachment and feels safe and protected, she develops the confidence that allows her to explore, try new things, and make mistakes. This confidence and willingness to experiment is what leads to competence as a young child and later as an adult. Developing secure attachments with parents and teachers results in competence and confidence, both now and later. When infant teachers make babies feel safe in the infant room, they are creating future confident learners for the preschool and kindergarten.

Years ago, the Harvard Preschool Project asserted that the time frame when humans develop the pattern they will continue to use to investigate new learning situations is set during the first nine months after developing independent mobility (for example, creeping, crawling, toddling). At the time they wrote, the researchers wcre connecting the information to physical competence and hands-on learning. Articles tracking the research encouraged parents and providers to get rid of playpens.

In this chapter, we will examine their conclusions in terms of intellectual and emotional competence. A self-fulfilling prophecy tells us that if people hear something or say it often enough, they begin to believe it as objective truth and act that belief out in their lives. When babies continually hear adults gasp in fear or tell them they are too little, that they can't, or no no no! or when they experience adults physically picking them up from behind to prevent crawling, climbing, or whatever the adult perceives as dangerous, it makes sense that a pattern of incompetence could result.

Attachment Theory, Confidence, and Competence

When Mary Ainsworth and John Bowlby originally engaged in their work on attachment, they struggled to find work on infants that could be scientifically documented. Both were certain that the quality of the adult-child relationship was as important to the whole picture as criteria that could be more easily documented. Bowlby's work with infants separated from their mothers and Ainsworth's work with the Strange Situation provided them with relationships for scientific investigation. We have come a long way since those times when interaction, context, and relationship were dismissed because of the challenges inherent in defining them. Because of the work of these theorists, it is now clear that understanding the quality of the relationships and interactions between babies and

Because of the work of these theorists, it is now clear that understanding the quality of the relationships and interactions between babies and their significant adults is critical to understanding their development.

their significant adults is critical to understanding their development. Nowhere is this clearer than in the connections between attachment and developing confidence and competence in babies.

It is sometimes challenging for teachers to make the connection between attachment and competence and confidence. I think this may be because we think of supporting attachment by encouraging connection, emotional safety, and interdependence, and we think of supporting competence and confidence by encouraging self-motivation, self-direction, and independence. Yet these qualities are quite interrelated. Each quality grows and feeds off the other. It is only when a baby has a sense of being safe, protected, and loved that she is able to take off independently to explore her world. Ainsworth's Strange Situation has demonstrated this time after time. When an infant has developed a secure attachment with a grown-up who keeps her safe from real harm and comforts her consistently when she is afraid, she can explore her world confidently.

Attachment Is Interactive

It may be easier to understand the connection between attachment and confidence and competence if you think of the way you react when stressed or fearful. Think of a situation or time when you felt unsafe. What was the cause of the feeling? A loud noise? An unexpected and violent summer storm? A narrowly averted automobile accident? How did you feel? Frightened? Alone? Horrified? Worried about your family's whereabouts?

What made you feel better? Perhaps you realized the source of the noise. Your partner came home and helped you secure the house from the impending storm. Your best friend came over, held your hand, and affirmed your feelings: "You must have been so scared!" You located your family members, and all felt right with the world. As adults, we already have skills and competence in many areas. But when we are afraid or under stress, we can still help ourselves feel more comfortable by getting the right information (the source of the noise, for example) or reaching out to someone we love and trust who can empathize with us.

Many of us have also had the experience of being in a very stressful situation in which the person we were with helped us to remain calm. Have you ever been lost in an unfamiliar city or country? If you were in the company of a calm, resourceful, competent friend, you were probably able to interact with each other in a way that made both of you feel better. Possibly you looked at a map together. Or perhaps she said, "There was an inn back there. We could go back and ask," or, "We're bound to run into other hikers—it will be okay!"

Or possibly you've experienced one of these scenarios with a friend who gave you even more to worry about. She might have said something like, "It looks like snow. It will be dark soon. We haven't passed a living being in forty minutes. There are probably bears! I wonder if those berries are poisonous. Do you believe in an afterlife?" This friend has no confidence in her ability to transcend the situation. She has no faith in your ability to transcend the situation. Gloom and doom give way to weeping or pacing. Even if you were originally feeling confident that you'd find a solution, at the very least your companion's state of mind added to the stress of your situation. Human beings have an effect on one another; our relationships are interactive.

Attachment is similar; it, too, is interactive. A constant relationship with a special adult gives the baby the opportunity to form an attachment. The baby's ability to develop confidence and competence is affected by what happens when the baby is with his special adult, just as the quality of a crisis is affected by the reactions of the friend involved. Have you ever been on a child care center playground on a gorgeous summer day, only to hear voices repeatedly saying, "No! No! No!" or, "You'll hurt yourself; you're going to fall"? Many adults unconsciously, in the name of safety, give children continual messages that they can't—just as the reactions of an anxious friend convey that there is really something to worry about.

Infant teachers continually transmit feelings of confidence or fear to the babies in their care. Most teachers are familiar with the following example: I'm sure you often explain to parents that when they hesitate at the door while their child is crying in the morning, they make it harder on the baby than if they confidently say, "I'm going to work now. I love you. I'll be back this afternoon, as always." Similarly, caregivers' attitudes tell babies whether they are safe to explore and whether the world around them can be trusted.

Most of us are afraid of something—storms, dogs, heights, water: the possibilities are endless. Often people experience fear because long ago they had an experience that was frightening, uncomfortable, or terrifying when they became separated from the special person whom they expected to keep them safe. Many such thoughts are subconscious. Most people don't even remember where they were when they were first frightened, but they know they have always been afraid of heights or fireworks. The power of our very earliest experiences is great. Our feelings of security or anxiety are frequently rooted in these unremembered early experiences. Similarly, our feelings of calm, safety, and confidence come from the interactions of our most important relationships. The quality of the attachment, or the relationship with the most important people in infants' lives, helps to determine whether they will approach new experiences with anxiety or confidence.

It is important to remember this as you go through your days with young children. You don't want them to become anxious about confidently exploring their safe surroundings. Your emotions serve as transmitters to the babies you care for, and they make a lasting impact on their confidence in the world around them. It's critical to reflect on the kinds of messages you routinely send.

Infant Competence

For a long time, adults paid little attention to infant competence. Babies' skills were underestimated for decades. It was only with the changing social context of the 1960s and the wealth of child development research that we began to reflect on our behaviors with infants and the effects of those behaviors on the developing child. It was then that Magda Gerber began to share the principles of her mentor, Emmi Pikler, whose life's work was encouraging babies to do all that they could do. It has been said that in Hungary people could spot a Pikler baby on the playground by the confidence and competence he demonstrated in his play. Gerber continued that important work when she came to America in the 1950s. Gerber's work in Southern California eventually resulted in establishing the first RIE (Resources for Infant Educaring) Infant Center in 1988 with her colleague, Tom Forest. The principles of RIE are still used in infant centers around the country, where Gerber's goal of fostering competent infants is helping parents to encourage confidence.

Magda Gerber points out that most adults tend to spend time with babies while preoccupied by other things. She believes that babies can entertain themselves for much longer periods of time if the adults who spend time with them offer their complete attention during that time. Gerber paved the way for today's parents and infant providers to view babies as competent. Her work demonstrates the interactive ways that parents, providers, and babies build one another's confidence and competence.

The importance of focusing on the interactive component of building confidence and competence cannot be repeated too frequently. Today, when it is becoming the norm for families to share the rearing of their children with other caregivers, it is essential for all of the adults to support and encourage each other. When their partnerships are strong, together they have a better chance of nurturing confident children.

Supporting Babies

When we support infants' attachment to the significant adults in their lives, we support their emerging confidence in themselves and their ability to get what they need from the people around them. This confidence in turn helps babies reach out for greater and greater competence as they explore their world. How can we support babies in their development of confidence and competence? Here's what attachment theory tells us:

- Infants need loving relationships. Food and shelter are not enough.

- Babies need stable significant relationships with a limited number of people; these do not need to be the biological parents.

- Babies probably benefit from a range of loving relationships right from the beginning.

- Consistency and continuity of care are important to developing infants.

One of the interesting things about these factors is that all, in their own way, defy principles that are deeply entrenched in our culture's way of looking at what babies need. Historically, the first relationship has been referred to as the mothering relationship. We now know that what babies need is competent physical care and loving, sensitive emotional care (or love, if you will). That care can come from biological mothers or fathers, adoptive parents, foster parents, grandparents, infant teachers, child care providers, or a favorite aunt, uncle, or family friend. The "who" is not nearly as important as the "how."

We also know that in the earliest weeks and months, a baby thrives best when the number of people in her life is limited to a few special, familiar faces. It is not best for babies to have a constantly changing cast of characters caring for her. We know from Bowlby's studies that the most competent caregivers, supplying food and clean diapers alone, cannot meet the necessary need of infants for love. If the carers are ever changing, the baby cannot establish the relationships necessary to develop trust in herself or others. It is relationships that make the difference in the infant's emotional well-being. This is why the early childhood community takes wages and benefits so seriously—we need to attract a strong, well-educated workforce of infant teachers to share the rearing of the next generation. We need to ensure that babies can count on the significant people with whom they share their earliest relationships.

The baby's relationships need to be loving and with a limited number of people. To say loving opens up a broad spectrum of relationships. It is probably easiest to describe a loving relationship with a new baby as one that includes a significant amount of holding, cuddling, and touch; a significant amount of eye contact, gazing, staring, and smiling; calm, affectionate feeding times, always in the arms of a caring grown-up; careful observation, which allows the caregiver to learn the baby's unique temperament; and finally, willingness on the part of each grown-up to compromise and work toward consensus with the baby's other significant adults to create caring, appropriate schedules and routines. We know that babies can and probably should be exposed to several important relationships, not just one.

Here are some of the barriers to providing loving relationships to new babies:

- Being afraid, as parents, that snuggling and kissing will spoil the baby.

- Being afraid, as providers, that snuggling and kissing will be considered unprofessional or inappropriate behavior.

- Letting policy issues take precedence over the importance of all of the grown-ups in a baby's life working together to support the baby. For example, a grandparent or provider may deny a pacifier to a baby whose mother is comfortable with this technique because she thinks she knows better than the parent what is best for the baby.

- Mothers monopolizing the care and nurturance of their infants rather than giving fathers or other significant adults the opportunity for developing close attachments.

- Hurried lifestyles that don't allow any of us to take the time to stare lovingly into the eyes of a newborn for extended periods of time.

Continuity of care is important. This does not mean that a baby cannot adapt to the different personality styles and approaches of Dad, Grandpa, Auntie, and infant provider or teacher. What it does mean is that the important adults in a baby's life need to talk to each other about what this particular baby needs in terms of daily care. Are the rituals for bedtime or mealtime discussed so the baby has the same wind-down techniques before sleeping and the same expectations for feeding from every adult? Do the baby's significant adults talk to each other about soothing techniques, diapering routines, and what the baby enjoys, is afraid of, and likes to play with? Do they keep each other informed about growth and developmental milestones, preferences, and dislikes? If the baby goes to sleep listening to favorite lullabies, is the same CD available at Auntie's? Babies learn to trust themselves and others by relying on the same routines, smiling faces, words of comfort, certain blankets. We cannot and would not want to arrange a perfect world for babies, but consistency in how the days and nights are spent is critical to helping them develop trust and attachment to the important people in their lives. In the end, that's what creates confident and competent babies and young children.

Supporting Families

The critical pieces of helping babies become themselves can be carried out by a variety of people—that much is clear. The success of the effort depends primarily on the relationships among the important adults in infants' lives. Even the tiniest babies absorb the emotional cues of the relationships around them. If the relationships are primarily tense and anxious, babies also feel tense and anxious. In infant child care, teachers' attitudes toward and relationships with parents are essential to helping babies develop confidence and competence.

The emotional tone of the relationship between parents and caregivers affects babies; in turn, the confidence instilled in parents by caregivers affects the relationship between parents and babies. For this reason, much of what will be discussed in this section is the need for collaboration among the important people who care for and about infants, and the infant caregiver's role in promoting that collaboration, even when it is difficult. Can parents and caregivers respect one another's differences? Can they agree to disagree? Can they listen to one another with respect? Can they jointly agree on an approach that everyone will try to implement for the sake of each baby, even if it means doing things in new ways that may be uncomfortable? Can infant teachers and child care providers realize that respect for parents' wishes is just as important as what they learned in child growth and development class? Both parents and caregivers have the power to affect this collaboration, but it is the caregiver's professional responsibility to foster it, regardless of the parents' attitudes and behavior. That is a tough truth about working with babies and families.

Experienced Parenthood

Being a parent is one of the most intense experiences life has to offer. It instills awe in those who, prior to giving birth, never quite understood what the big deal was. Those of us who have worked as mothers and early educators can usually remember the trepidation with which we approached diarrhea, vomiting, and high fevers in our workplace before having children. How could this become an ordinary task that didn't feel burdensome or a little scary? How could anyone involve herself in this process, much less clean up afterward automatically? Often we're not sure when or how the transition took place and the feelings of experienced parenthood settled in.

It is important to talk a little about the feelings of experienced parenthood because very few people do. Like falling in love with a partner and not quite being able to describe it, baby love, too, takes parents by surprise. Parents are surprised by how wonderful it is. They are also surprised by how stressful and awful it can sometimes be. They find it difficult to discuss either end of the spectrum of feelings. I don't know a mother who can honestly say it is just what she expected. Usually people have expectations that it will be wonderful, and then they are surprised by how much deeper and more complex their feelings for their children are.

I use the word *experienced* because usually it takes awhile to feel the feelings of parenthood. It is often distressing to a new mother, for example, when she does not immediately feel deep tenderness for her baby. It is also deeply distressing to new parents to see their baby in distress and not be able to alleviate his pain. For parents whose babies are of a challenging temperament or for whom the match of temperament between baby and parent is not easy, it can be especially painful.

The emotional tone of the relationship between parents and caregivers affects babies; in turn, the confidence instilled in parents by caregivers affects the relationship between parents and babies.

It is a humbling day of reckoning for most parents when the myths and reality clash for the first time. The way these feelings are managed, or not managed, is the stuff that attachment for parents and children is made of. In turn, the attachment that results from those feelings fosters confidence and competence in the new parents and the baby.

Mother Blaming and Infant Care Providers

Unfortunately, the legacy of the psychoanalytic community, primarily one of mother blaming, provides another source of difficulty between providers and parents. This tendency, left over from psychological thinking of fifty to a hundred years ago, infects the way domestic issues around employment and child care are presented to us every day. We do not see headlines describing the risk to children of employed fathers. We rarely hear strangers say, "Well, where was the father when the accident happened?" We talk about the increased risk of teenage pregnancy, which rises between the hours of 3:00 and 6:00 pm, when *mothers* have not yet returned from work. Why do we not equally say when *fathers* are not at home? It is true that in a culture striving for continual political correctness, we are more likely to hear the word *parents* than we were thirty years ago, but all mothers know that for the most part, *parents* means mothers.

Jim Greenman, author of *Prime Times*, Janet Gonzalez Mena, author of *Diversity in Early Care and Education*, Alice Honig, and others have pointed out that this very biased mother blaming finds its way into the professional early childhood field as well. Just as mothers feel there is not enough honesty among women about the true demands and dilemmas of mothering, a certain silence exists in the early childhood field about the antagonism sometimes expressed in subtle and not-so-subtle ways to the parents of children in our care. Many early childhood professionals have eloquently tried to address the situation. In 1980, for example, Lilian Katz outlined the ways in which parents and providers do and ought to differ in their approach to children (Katz 1980).

Distinctions between Mothering and Teaching in Their Central Tendencies on Seven Dimensions

Role Dimension	Mothering	Teaching
1. Scope of functions	Diffuse and limitless	Specific and limited
2. Intensity of affection	High	Low
3. Attachment	Optimum attachment	Optimum detachment
4. Rationality	Optimum irrationality	Optimum rationality
5. Spontaneity	Optimum spontaneity	Optimum intentionality
6. Partiality	Partial	Impartial
7. Scope of responsibility	Individual	Whole group

We have courses in ECE college preparation that discuss the importance of parent involvement. We talk about respecting the

131

culture and ethnicity of the families we serve. We talk about parents as their child's first teachers. We learn that we need to adjust our approach to an infant based on his family's desire for care. Still, ask yourself if you have ever heard any of the following in your workplace or from teachers at a conference or during a day of professional development:

- Why do they even bother having children when they just dump them on us eleven hours a day?

- Can you believe she wants us to put her on the potty? That baby is ten months old! That woman needs her head examined!

- You're right! It's not the kids that give us problems—it's the parents!

- I can't believe she would ask me who bit her baby! Hasn't she ever heard of confidentiality?

- I don't care what they did in her home country. This is America, and we don't breast-feed two-year-olds.

- He expects me to carry that baby around all day. I swear that's what they do all weekend. Our Mondays with her are always so hard. It takes us three days to get her back in our routine; then it's the weekend, and the parents mess her up again!

- She has such a hard time separating from that baby. She's going to be sorry. I've told her the baby is just fine as soon as she leaves.

- She comes in here in her expensive business suit, holding that infant like he's a sack of potatoes. It would be a tragedy if he spit up on her and she had to look like us all day!

- I happen to know she gets out of work at four! She comes rushing in here at 5:29, when she knows we close at 5:30. What has she been doing all afternoon?

- Jenna said she had her bathing suit on under her shirt. She saw it. That poor baby! Mom has a day off and leaves her with us so she can go to the beach? She shouldn't have had a baby if she doesn't want to be with one!

The resentment expressed in comments like these is far from unusual in early childhood settings. It is even understandable when we reflect on all the things that divide caregivers from parents, including class, culture, education, income, age, and a host of other factors. However, if this resentment is allowed to fester unacknowledged and undiscussed, caregivers may consciously or unconsciously act on it. This has a huge impact not only on caregivers' relationships with parents but also on the babies, whom caregivers instinctively want to protect. It is not possible to provide really good care for babies while carrying this level of resentment of their parents.

Providing Emotional Support

It is clear that raising a child is a huge responsibility. Most parents readily admit it is much more involved, intense, and complicated than they had ever anticipated. Most parents also suggest that they find that people who are not focused on the lives and needs of babies believe child rearing is a pretty easy piece of work. This is one of the barriers to feeling confident as a parent or caregiver. When there is a disconnect between the complexity of the work and the perceptions of others about the complexity of the work, a person is set up for feelings of incompetence. And remember, if parents feel incompetent or afraid or anxious, these feelings are communicated to the baby. Clearly, a primary part of a caregiver's job is helping parents develop confidence in their own instincts, decisions, and knowledge of their babies.

One of Brazelton's mentors was the English writer and parent educator D.W. Winnicott. Winnicott spent years doing radio programs aimed at helping parents understand the job of raising a child. He was one of the first to talk about the concept of "good enough" parenting. He disliked the words *parent education* because he thought they were somewhat condescending. In his 1971 volume, *Talking to Parents*, he writes, "Any kind of propaganda, or telling people what to do, is to be deplored. It is an insult to indoctrinate people, even for their own good, unless they have the chance by being present to react, to express disapproval, and to contribute."

Winnicott believed that when you can show people what they are doing in a positive light, they become less afraid. People seek information, and parents want to do well by their children. Like Brazelton, Winnicott believed that Western culture does not do enough to help or empathize with new parents. He was always very aware that parents are forced to make many quick decisions. Some of those decisions are going to be wrong, and we need to help parents see that they can only do the best they can do at the time that they do it. If parents and caregivers work together, everyone can reflect on situations and learn from the many mistakes we are all bound to make.

This is part of what I would consider a definition of experienced parenting—or indeed, experienced caregiving. It means coming to terms with the fact that every day you have to get up and be there for your child, making decisions—some of which will be wrong— and get up again the next day, understanding that fact but enthusiastically embracing the job anyway. It means being able to forgive yourself and move on. It means accepting that your partner lets the baby eat ice cream with chocolate syrup . . . and she will probably still live a healthy life! It means accepting that you are a single parent and you are all your baby needs right now. It means having confidence in your ability to rear your child, even though you will make many mistakes. Caregivers are on the front lines in helping parents develop this confidence.

Winnicott proposes to parents that we are all inclined to be too idealistic when we ponder creating a life for a child. He cautions parents against striving for perfection and expecting it in their experience as parents. Yet many caregivers continue to act as if there is such a thing as perfect parents. Early childhood teachers continue to hold parents, particularly mothers, to standards that they are unlikely to achieve in the real world.

The extent to which this perfectionism and mythology affects each generation cannot be overstated. As Brazelton writes in *Touchpoints* (1992), "Parents receiving support for their emotions and efforts are in a better position to recognize and promote the healthy steps towards both dependence and independence in their children." Brazelton, whose experience working with both infants and their families spans decades, believes that parents who feel supported through their baby's developmental transitions are much better able to support their infants than parents who are socially isolated or lack support. He believes that providers who are able to avoid the old top-down approach to educating parents can empower parents by sharing with them how their approaches contribute to their child's growth and mastery of his world. These providers respectfully rely on the parents as the adults who know this baby best.

Different Right Ways

Perhaps there is no greater challenge to working with other people's children than knowing that a child is being hurt by her parents. There are a few circumstances in which everyone who cares about children has a responsibility to intervene. It's important at the same time to understand the difference between abuse and neglect, on the one hand, and child-rearing practices that may be related to class, culture, or family, on the other. Many times educators are caught between doing what they have been trained to consider best practice and following a parent's wishes for his child's care. For example, in my recent experience in New Hampshire, I found that it is not unusual for families new to this country to request that their baby and toddler be allowed to sleep together at rest time. In many states, this would violate licensing regulations. Yet if we think about it, children are comforted by other people, just as they are by teddies or special blankets, which we routinely include in a child's napping routine.

Similarly, practices such as allowing children to have a bottle or pacifier, breast-feeding children into their preschool years, keeping babies constantly in carriers close to their mothers' bodies, or allowing babies and young children to cosleep with parents are all unusual in independence-oriented American society, but these practices do not qualify as neglect or abuse. If you take parents' requests seriously and understand their importance to the children and the families involved, you will do the best you can to find a way to honor them. It is possible to get a variance from most licensing regulations if you can show why the exception serves children and families and what you are doing to keep children safe.

Everyone who works with babies and families has to try hard to see things from multiple perspectives. In a culture that offers little to young families in terms of societal support, infant caregivers can have a huge and positive influence on the future by supporting the parents of the next generation. Infant teachers can aid parents of babies in their care by helping them feel as confident as possible. How different a young parent will feel going off to work in those earliest weeks of care when her child's teacher says, "You can feel great about all this fretting and crying. It's proof of her growing attachment to you!" rather than, "Go ahead to work—she's always fine as soon as you leave!"

We know that confident babies grow under the nurturance of competent parents. So the bottom line for infant teachers who care passionately about the babies in their care is remembering that every sincere compliment that helps a parent feel confident results in the gift of competence for the baby as well.

Communication Is Paramount

Without the benefit of scientific research on my side, I want to present some "grandmother's gut" ideas drawn from my memories of early motherhood, conversations with new moms today, and forty years of observations and experience working in the early childhood field:

- Motherhood (parenthood) is as startling and earthshaking an experience today as it has always been.

- Despite the volumes of research and how-to baby books that line the shelves of bookstores, new parents continue to feel intimidated and awed by the complexity of caring for a newborn.

- The job is both more complicated and complex, as well as more rewarding and wonderful, than any of us ever imagined.

- Most mothers feel at least a little bit insulted by the notion promoted in American culture by those who have not had children that it is a relatively easy job we should all be doing more successfully.

- Just as mothers resent preconceived notions about mothering from those who haven't tried it, nonmothers resent a perceived "secret club" that everyone seems to automatically enter upon becoming a parent.

- Many early educators resent the notion that being a parent gives someone a different perspective on child development than one can get from a degree program in ECE.

- Acknowledging one's own lack of experience as a parent makes building a relationship with new parents easier for the teacher and more supportive for the parents.

- This topic of education/experience is one that has always been uncomfortable for people in the early childhood field and the general public as well.

- A teacher's degree in child growth and development gives her important information that a parent may not have, just as family life with a baby gives a parent a perspective that a teacher may not have.

- People who have children and those who do not have an awkward time discussing most of these issues.

- If parents and nonparents can talk more openly about this, the result will be better relationships and better care for babies.

For as long as I can remember, there have been very tender feelings between mothers and nonmothers, fathers and nonfathers, teachers who are also parents and teachers who are not, and child care providers who have degrees and child care providers who do not. For as long as I can remember, women (mostly grandmothers) reflecting on years of raising children can laugh at themselves for all of the thoughts they had about raising children—until they actually started having them. I saw a book recently that I wish I had thought to write—*I Was a Great Parent until I Became One*! For many years, I have been able to react calmly and maturely when people suggest I could be a better teacher/writer/housekeeper/cook—but criticize my parenting, and I either launch into lioness mode or drop into deep depression. I know I am not alone in this—and it's a lifelong challenge. I also know it is related in some complicated way to this whole topic of confidence and competence and how we do or don't nurture it in one another. I also know if we could figure it out and integrate it into our parenting and teaching practices, we would be better at preparing the next generation for all they have ahead of them.

It is my hunch that most of you reading these words will quietly nod your head in agreement. Yet in reality this is still a pretty big issue for those of us in the early childhood field and those living family lives. For example, how many of the following statements have a familiar ring to you?

- I don't mind when my mother criticizes my meatloaf, but when she talks about the kids, it makes me crazy!

- I'd much rather hire someone with experience than one of those college girls who comes in here with a lot of book learning but doesn't know how to act with the toddlers.

- That woman thinks just because I don't have children, I don't know anything about them. She could learn so much from me if she'd just listen.

- You know, I can deal so well with her tantrums at home, but when she flies into one at the end of the day at child care, I wish I could just run away.

- I applied for that job as director, and I didn't get it. I've been here for fourteen years, and I know the center, the staff, and the families, but they hired that young woman just because she has a graduate degree in child care administration!

- We used to be such good friends, but we don't see each other that much anymore. All she talks about is that baby. Nothing has ever been so important! It makes me sad.

- We used to be such good friends, but we don't see each other that much anymore. I'm still carting baby fat. She always looks gorgeous. She's in court solving major legal issues. I'm at the Y, doing baby swim and gym! It makes me sad.

Sorting through which issues are complex and which are complicated—not to mention which are a little of both—is no small task. Beginning the conversation is a simple way to start. Nurturing confidence in babies, their parents, and their primary caregivers is also bound to create competence in the next generation.

Attachment Theory and Public Policy

We have now looked at many theories of infant and attachment development. The impact of these theories has been discussed in terms of families and society. For parents and educators, the critical element in all this is its implications for practice. What good is this information? How can it help us be better child care providers, infant teachers, parents, aunties, or grandparents? Or for that matter, how can it help us be better decision makers, citizens, child advocates, or voters? Urie Bronfenbrenner has outlined for us the importance of context to rearing the next generation. He suggests that perhaps government policies, community development, global patterns, and international affairs will affect the developing child far more deeply than a maternal choice about breast- or bottle-feeding (1979). No longer should we look to a baby's mother as the all-encompassing source of infant well-being or lack thereof.

Motherhood is still up there with apple pie and patriotism. Yet in the United States there is little or no attempt to put our money where our mouths are when it comes to supporting those who rear the next generation. Policies to support young families are next to nonexistent in this country. The Family Leave Act is the first legislation to reach out to parents at all, and it is only helpful to those in affluent enough circumstances to take time off without pay when a child comes into the family. How does public policy affect new families? For a start, consider the impact on attachment, confidence, and competence of these factors, all shaped by public policy:

- Excessive fatigue on the part of parents due to inadequate government policies to support young families (brief or nonexistent parental leave policies)

- Lack of adequate financial or human resources to support the new family

- Turnover rates in infant care centers that are far too high because of working conditions and inadequate compensation

- Child care policies in infant centers that put efficiency of routines above primary caregiving

What do we need? Families and providers can work together to change the way our society supports young families and child care providers. Parents and caregivers can be on each other's side. Here are some changes in public policy that would better support attachment and ensure loving relationships for newborns:

- Adequate parental leave for all new parents

- More community and societal support of young families

- Required courses in high school on child development and sociology of the family

139

- More training for early educators on the importance of family support to one's job description

- Higher pay, better overall compensation, and improved working conditions for child care providers

We all have a role to play in increasing society's respect for young babies and the parents and child care providers who nurture them. We can change our own practices and our own behavior, and we can advocate for changes in public policy. Attachment in babies and confident and competent parents, providers, and young children can be created only when we accept the necessity of changing ourselves and public policy. Attachment theory can help us explain to politicians, media representatives, and the general public why these changes are crucial. Babies, and their families, deserve no less.

Discussion Questions

1. Magda Gerber says most of us are preoccupied when we spend time with the babies in our care. Are you? How do you know? If so, what can you do about it?

2. What are your strategies for nurturing competence in new parents when you strongly disagree with their priorities for their baby? Who do you rely on to help you with the choices made to support this family?

3. Have you ever engaged in the "mother blaming" so common in our field? What were the circumstances? What might you have done differently? What resources do you use to make your decisions?

Suggestions for Further Reading

Kendall-Tackett, Kathleen A. 2001. *The hidden feelings of motherhood: Coping with stress, depression, and burnout.* Oakland, CA: New Harbinger Publications, Inc.

Stonehouse, Anne. 1995. *How does it feel? Child care from a parent's perspective.* Redmond, WA: Exchange Press.

Winnicott, D. W. 1971. *Talking to parents.* Reading, MA: Addison-Wesley Publishing Company.

active listening: The process of repeating what has been said to clarify what we have heard and understood.

active participant: The concept that babies need to become part of their routines, not to passively receive them.

anxious-ambivalent insecure attachment: A type of attachment where the child tends to express distress when near strangers or unfamiliar settings, whether the parent or caregiver is nearby or not; child exhibits extreme anxiety and distress when the parent departs, but, is often resistant to reuniting when the parent returns.

anxious-avoidant insecure attachment: A type of attachment where the infant lacks affect and shows little emotional response toward adults, regardless of whether they are parents, primary caregivers, or strangers.

attachment: An enduring emotional bond or connection between people, often focusing on the bond between infants and their parents of caregivers.

basic trust: The understanding that a child needs to be an initiator, explorer, and self-learner.

bonding: The process of forming an attachment.

consistency: Following the same pattern or doing things in the same manner each time.

cross-cultural research: Similar or identical research performed on the same topics in different countries or within different cultural settings.

denial: Refusal to look at the reality of a situation in an objective manner.

detachment: A parent's refusal or avoidance of getting to close to his or her child because the parent fears separation.

educarer: A person who cares for children as they educate or educates while providing care; term coined by Magda Gerber.

environment: The physical space and emotional situation in which a child or infant exists.

lifespan development: The physical and emotional development a person goes through in a lifetime; lifespan development is believed to be strongly affected during infancy.

looping: In early childhood education, the practice whereby a teacher remains with a group of children as they grow; also the practice whereby a teacher works with different age groups every several years.

Neonatal Behavioral Assessment Scale (NBAS): An assessment instrument that uses information obtained from providing newborns with visual, auditory and tactile stimuli to study their responses to the environment; developed by T. Berry Brazelton and colleagues.

overstimulate: Exposing an infant or child to too many physical, sensory, or emotional experiences at once; exposing an infant or child to overly strong experiences.

projection: Transferring one's feelings or experiences to others.

RIE: Resourses for Infant Educaring; established by Magda Gerber.

second-stage bonding: A second stage of attachment, occurring over the first several months of an infant's life offering parents and babies opportunities to develop relationships if the initial opportunity had been lost to medical or other emergency situations.

secure attachment: An attachment where the infant or child feels safe and protected consistently; attachment theorists believe that secure attachments in infancy and early childhood are important for individuals to develop healthy future relationships.

separation anxiety: A child's or infant's fear or nervousness caused by the thought or fact of being separated from a parent or other primary caregiver.

sensitive observation: Carefully watching and listening to an infant to determine or understand the child's needs.

Strange Situation: A twenty-minute observation of infant play in an unfamiliar room while both familiar and unfamiliar adults enter and leave the room. Developed by Mary Ainsworth, its purpose is to determine a child's attachment behaviors.

stranger anxiety: A child's or infant's fear or unease when encountering or being exposed to new people.

strength-based: Focusing observation or assessment on what is going well, as opposed to what is going wrong.

uninterrupted play: Long periods of time when infants are allowed to play on their own at their own pace without adult intervention.

warm line: A non-emergency telephone resource for individuals needing support or information (as opposed to an emergency hot line).

Ainsworth, Mary. 1967. *Infancy in Uganda: infant care and the growth of love.* Baltimore: Johns Hopkins Press.

Berger, Kathleen Stassen. 2001. *The developing person through the life span.* New York: Worth Publishers.

Bowlby, John. 1940. The influence of early environment in the development of neurosis and neurotic character. *International Journal of Psychoanalysis* 21:154–78.

———. 1951. *Maternal care and mental health.* Geneva: World Health Organization.

———. 1958. *Can I leave my baby?* London: National Association for Mental Health.

———. 1967. Foreword to *Infancy in Uganda: Infant care and the growth of love,* by Mary Ainsworth. Baltimore: Johns Hopkins Press.

———. 1970. *Child care and the growth of love.* 2nd ed. Baltimore: Penguin.

———. 1973. *Separation.* Vol. 2 of *Attachment and loss.* New York: Basic.

———. 1980. *Loss: Sadness and depression.* Vol. 3 of *Attachment and loss.* New York: Basic.

———. 1982. *Attachment.* Vol. 1 of *Attachment and loss.* New York: Basic.

Brazelton, T. Berry. 1969. *Infants and mothers: Differences in development.* New York: Dell Publishing Company.

———. 1981. *On becoming a family.* New York: Delacorte Press.

———. 1983. *Infants and mothers: Differences in development.* Rev. ed. New York: Delacorte Press.

———. 1985. *Working and caring.* Reading, MA: Addison-Wesley Publishing Company.

———. 1992. *Touchpoints: Your child's emotional and behavioral development.* Reading, MA: Addison-Wesley Publishing Company.

Brazelton, T. Berry, and Joshua D. Sparrow. 2003. *Discipline the Brazelton way.* Cambridge, MA: Perseus Publishing.

Bronfenbrenner, Urie. 1979. *The ecology of human development.* Cambridge, MA: Harvard University Press.

Caldwell, Bettye M., and Asa G. Hilliard. 1985. *What is quality child care?* Washington, DC: National Association for the Education of Young Children.

Copple, Carol, and Natalie Cavanaugh. 2003. *A world of difference: Readings on teaching young children in a diverse society.* Washington, DC: National Association for the Education of Young Children.

References

Crittenden, Ann. 2001. *The price of motherhood: Why the most important job in the world is still the least valued.* New York: Henry Holt and Company.

Douglas, Susan J., and Meredith W. Michaels. 2005. *The mommy myth: The idealization of motherhood and how it has undermined women.* New York: Free Press.

Erikson, Erik. 1968. *Identity: Youth and crisis.* New York: W.W. Norton & Company.

Fraiberg, Selma. 1977. *Every child's birthright.* New York: Basic Books.

Gandini, Lella, and Carolyn Pope Edwards, eds. 2001. *Bambini: The Italian approach to infant/toddler care.* New York: Teachers College Press.

Gerber, Magda. 2002. *Dear parent: Caring for infants with respect.* Los Angeles: Resources for Infant Educarers.

Gesell, Arnold, Frances L. Ilg, and Louise Bates Ames. 1943. *Infant and child in the culture of today.* New York: Harper and Row.

Gonzalez-Mena, Janet. 1993. *Multicultural issues in child care.* Mountain View, CA: Mayfield Publishing Company.

———. 2007. *Diversity in early care and education.* New York: McGraw-Hill.

Greenman, Jim, Anne Stonehouse, and Gigi Schweikert. 2008. *Prime times.* St. Paul, MN: Redleaf Press.

Halfon, Neal, Kathryn Taaffe McLearn, and Mark A. Schuster, eds. 2002. *Child rearing in America: Challenges facing parents with young children.* New York: Cambridge University Press.

Hast, Fran, and Ann Hollyfield. 1999. *Infant and toddler experiences.* St. Paul, MN: Redleaf Press.

Honig, Alice Sterling. 2002. *Secure relationships: Nurturing infant/toddler attachment in early care settings.* Washington, DC: National Association for the Education of Young Children.

Jervis, Kathe, ed. 1999. *Separation: Strategies for helping two- to four-year-olds.* Washington, DC: National Association for the Education of Young Children.

Kagan, Jerome. 1998. *Three seductive ideas.* Cambridge, MA: Harvard University Press.

Karen, Robert. 1998. *Becoming attached: First relationships and how they shape our capacity to love.* New York: Oxford University Press.

Katz, Lilian. 1980. Mothering and teaching. In Vol. 3 of Current topics in early childhood education. Norwood, NJ: Ablex.

Karr-Morse, Robin, and Meredith S. Wiley. 1997. *Ghosts from the nursery: Tracing the roots of violence.* New York: The Atlantic Monthly Press.

Kendall-Tackett, Kathleen A. 2001. *The hidden feelings of motherhood: Coping with stress, depression, and burnout.* Oakland, CA: New Harbinger Publications, Inc.

Klaus, Marshall H., and John H. Kennell. 1976. *Maternal-infant bonding: The impact of early separation or loss on family development.* Saint Louis: Mosby.

Leach, Penelope. 1978. *Your baby and child: From birth to age five.* New York: Alfred A. Knopf.

Leboyer, Frederick. 1995. *Birth without violence.* Rochester, VT: Inner Traditions Publishers.

Madrid, Antonio, and Dale Pennington. 2000. Maternal-infant bonding and asthma. *Journal of Prenatal and Perinatal Psychology and Health* 14 (314): 279–290.

Mangione, Peter. 1988. *Respectfully yours: Magda Gerber's approach to professional infant/toddler care.* Video magazine. Sacramento, CA: California Department of Education.

Mercer, Jean. 2006. *Understanding attachment.* Westport, CT: Praeger Publishers.

Nilsson, Lennart. 1980. *A child is born.* New York: Delacorte Press.

Papousek, M., M. Schieche, and H. Wurmser. 2008. *Disorders of behavioral and emotional regulation in the first years of life: Early risks and intervention in the developing parent-infant relationship.* Washington, DC: Zero to Three.

Petrie, Stephanie, and Sue Owen. 2006. *Authentic relationships in group care for infants and toddlers: Resources for infant educarers (RIE) principles into practice.* London and Philadelphia: Jessica Kingsley Publishers.

Piaget, Jean. 1976. *The child and reality.* New York: Penguin Books.

Schaffer, Rudolph. 1978. *Mothering.* Cambridge, MA: Harvard University Press.

Sears, William, and Martha Sears. 2001. *Attachment parenting.* Boston: Little, Brown.

Smith, Janna Malamud. 2003. *A Potent spell: Mother love and the power of fear.* Boston and New York: Houghton Mifflin Company.

Spock, Benjamin. 1970. *Baby and child care.* New York: Pocket Books.

Stern, Daniel. 1977. *The first relationships: Infant and mother.* Cambridge, MA: Harvard University Press.

Stonehouse, Anne. 1994. *How does it feel? Child care from a parent's perspective.* Canberra: Australian Early Childhood Association.

Thomas, A., S. Chess, and H. G. Birch. 1968. *Temperament and behavior disorder in children.* New York: University Press.

Viorst, Judith. 1998. *Necessary losses: The loves, illusions, dependencies, and impossible expectations that all of us have.* New York: Free Press.

References

Warner, Judith. 2005. *Perfect madness: Motherhood in the age of anxiety.* New York: Riverhead Books.

Warren, Rita. 1977. *Caring: Supporting children's growth.* Washington, DC: National Association for the Education of Young Children.

Weber, Susan. 2003. The lives and work of Emmi Pikler and Magda Gerber. *Gateway* (Spring/Summer): 4–9. New York: Pocket Books.

Winnicott, D. W. 1971. *Talking to parents.* Reading, MA: Addison-Wesley Publishing Company.

Wolpert, Ellen. 2005. *Start seeing diversity: The basic guide to an anti-bias classroom.* St. Paul, MN: Redleaf Press.

Zero to Three Journal. 2008. Washington, DC: Zero to Three.

Index

Index